A Zone of Nonbeing

A Black Pole's Reflections on Racism in Poland

Christian Kobluk

Daraja Press

Published by
Daraja Press
https://darajapress.com

© 2025 Christian Kobluk

Cover design: Kate McDonnell

ISBN: 978-1-998309-43-6 soft cover
ISBN: 978-1-998309-43-6 ebook

EU Safety Information

Publisher: Daraja Press, PO Box 99900 BM 735 664, Wakefield, QC J0X 0C2, Canada
info@darajapress.com | https://darajapress.com
EU Authorized GPSR Representative: Easy Access System Europe
Mustamäe tee 50, 10621 Tallinn, Estonia, gpsr.requests@easproject.com
For EU product safety concerns, please contact us at info@darajapress.com

Library and Archives Canada Cataloguing in Publication

Title: A zone of nonbeing : a black Pole's reflections on racism in Poland / Christian Kobluk.
Names: Kobluk, Christian, author.
Description: Includes bibliographical references.
Identifiers: Canadiana (print) 20250117290 | Canadiana (ebook) 20250117320 | ISBN 9781998309429 (softcover) | ISBN 9781998309436 (EPUB)
Subjects: LCSH: Black people—Poland—History. | LCSH: Racism—Poland—History. | LCSH: Anti-racism— Poland—History. | LCSH: Poland—Race relations—History.
Classification: LCC DK4121.5.B53 K63 2025 | DDC 943.8/00496—dc23

*The ability of writers to imagine what is not the self,
to familiarize the strange and mystify the familiar,
is the best test of their power.*

Toni Morrison

*There is a zone of nonbeing, an extraordinary sterile and arid region,
an utterly naked declivity where an authentic upheaval can be born.*

Franz Fanon

*Not everything that is faced can be changed;
but nothing can be changed until it is faced.*

James Baldwin

*For all fighters for equality and freedom
all around the world*

An Open Secret	ix
PART ONE	
Blacks and Poles	1
On the Myth of Clean Hands	7
Encounter with Communism	14
PART TWO	
Memories of a Student, Thoughts of a Teacher	22
The Price of a Ticket	26
A Zone of Nonbeing	38
PART THREE	
Keep It Quiet	48
Jimmy's Room	55
Time to Wake Up My Nation	59
Trouble Don't Last Always	65
Acknowledgments	73
Bibliography	75

An Open Secret

When I finished *Notes of a Black Pole* (*Zapiski czarnego Polaka*) in October 2022, I was still incredibly unaware of racial struggles in Poland. Moreover, I did not yet understand that I was probably one of the first—if not the very first—Black Polish essayists to speak about racism in my country in the Polish language. I even found it bizarre that my book-length debut has been mostly about the color of my skin.

Two years earlier, I was one of the co-organizers of the Black Lives Matter protest in my home city. This was my first encounter with the racial struggle, which has been taking place all around the world. It does not obviously mean, I've never faced racism before, but rather I haven't seen it as part of a bigger, worldwide issue or system.

Toward the end of 2022, after conversations with my African and Afropean friends who had encouraged me to translate my book, I started to think more about *this*. What does it really mean to be Polish and Black? What does Polish racism look like? What does it mean to be Black in this country during the migration crisis? I've been thinking, speaking, and writing about these questions ever since. I've been explaining—sometimes successfully, sometimes not—*my* situation to my (chiefly white) Polish acquaintances and friends, and I've had to notice that, in numerous instances, they didn't understand me at all. It has been as if I've spoken a completely unknown language. But there was—and is—goodwill after all. I recall a conversation with my high school English and Latin teacher who—after reading my essays—asked, "Have I ever said something inappropriate?" The point was, I think, "Now I understand better how deep the roots of our racism are, and I understand I could have unconsciously made a mistake." Well, that's not a common reaction.

I thought I could find something in Johny Pitts' *Afropean*. He wrote about Sheffield, Paris, and Saint-Paul-de-Venice; about Marseille and the French Riviera; about Brussels and Amsterdam; about Stockholm and Berlin; about Rome and Lisbon. There is even a chapter about Russia! But nothing about Warsaw, Kraków, Wrocław, or Poznań. It's not an accusation of any kind. (Especially since he openly says, "Some big capital cities, particularly in Eastern and Southern Europe, such as Vienna, *Warsaw*, [...] and Madrid, are also absent [...] of the work than I would have liked."[1]) I'm just trying to

---

1 Johny Pitts, *Afropean*, 9.

illustrate how deeply buried the issue of racism in Poland is. Well, we did not have any colonies in Africa, Asia, or the Americas (at least, not officially). We have not had any history of Black slaves. Poland is still quite a monoethnic country. One doesn't see many non-whites in the streets. That is why I believe we do not notice our racism.

Furthermore, Poland is a relatively secure country. There haven't been any terrorist attacks (I can remember a few attempts, though), any mass shootings in schools, or any Ku Klux Klan. Something like the U.S. Capitol attack in 2021 would be almost unthinkable here. Scarcely any person carries a gun; police, compared to American police, are almost gentle.

But at the same time, it doesn't mean that we are in a completely safe state or that Polish racism does not exist. The last one just has a different form and is harder to notice and, therefore, to eradicate. This is an open secret of a kind. Ultimately, since we haven't had any Jim Crow, we've had no Martin Luther King Jr. or Malcolm X either.

I should, nevertheless, add that I love my country. I am not ashamed of my Polishness; moreover, I cherish it. I know the history of my motherland very well, and I admire its culture and find its cuisine great. I sing and stand for our national anthem, and when I hear patriotic songs, my heart beats faster. I *am* Pole—there's no doubt about it.

Nonetheless, I *am* also Black. I fear going out on Independence Day. I know very well—too well, I should say—that my co-patriots usually do not consider me, at least at first, to be Polish. It does not matter if I was born *here*, if I speak *our language*, or if I know *our culture*. For them, the color of my skin is a clear indication that I *am* a foreigner.

The other thing that should be explained is, since it is a book for English-language readers, the differences between Polish and English racial slurs and descriptions. That will be a topic explored during our journey, yet now, I shall condense it. First, there is still a quite popular term, "Murzyn," which can be translated as "Negro." Until 2020, it was commonly considered a neutral description of any Black. Only after the murder of George Floyd, the debate has begun on whether it might be offensive. In 2020, the Council for the Polish Language (Rada Języka Polskiego), the official language regulating the institution of Polish, suggested that "Murzyn" should be considered derogatory. Also, the official Polish dictionary now states that

"Murzyn" is offensive.[2] Despite this, many of my co-citizens do not acknowledge this position. Second, the word which can be admitted as the equivalent of "Nigger" is "czarnuch." On that one, everyone agrees, it is a racial slur in its purest form used exclusively as such. We also have the term "Afropolak" ("Afro-Pole" or "African Pole"), yet it is not widely used, as far as I know.

I believe it was James Baldwin—one of my heroes—who said that the hardest thing one can do is to face fellow travelers of some sort. I couldn't agree more. Writing this book, I have felt I am betraying my own nation in some sense. I think, however, that true love is not simple and thoughtless admiration—sometimes it is also harsh critique. Love *is* a terrifying thing.

That is one of the reasons I wrote *Notes of a Black Pole* and, partially, this book. It is about improving my nation. If we, the Polish people, can see our flaws, perhaps we will also be able to change ourselves.

The second reason is that I've wanted to explain to my Black brothers and sisters who live in Poland and don't speak Polish yet what it means to be Black in this country. This book is a sort of answer to those who have asked me to translate *Notes*. It is for those Blacks in Poland who are foreigners and want to know about whispers, racial politics, and propaganda of fear.

The third reason is to show, especially my fellow Afropeans, that *we*, the Black Poles, exist. We're not unicorns or other fantastic creatures. Racial struggle in Europe does not take place only in this part of the continent widely referred to as the Western one. It *is* different, there's no doubt, but it *exists*. Perhaps I am wrong, but I cannot resist the feeling that so-called "Black studies" have not yet included my part of Europe. We're still *terra incognita,* the unknown land. It's time to change it.

And last but not least, I feel something that was called by Baldwin "a burden of representation." I *am* a Black citizen of Poland, and these essays are an attempt—perhaps an unsuccessful one—to make sense of that. Not for anyone, but for me—and me alone. Long story short, I'm trying—quite desperately, I should add—to find myself: like in any other book I wrote (and I will have written) about what we call "race."

Nobody, especially Blacks who were raised among only whites, can really understand their own identity. For someone like me, who has been told

---

2 See: Słownik języka polskiego PWN, https://sjp.pwn.pl/sjp/murzyn;2485162.html

almost their entire life that the West is the *only* civilization worth knowing and the Euro-American history is the *only* history of the world, it's even harder. I did not have *my* Frederick Douglass, Frantz Fanon, James Baldwin, Toni Morrison, Angela Davis, or Maya Angelou. I was created, mostly, by Poland and Europe. Those places have "woven me out of thousand details, anecdotes [and] stories..."[3] as Fanon says. For most of my life, I have been completely unable to say I am Black or, the most, what it means.

I can no longer pretend that I did not hear through the grapevine about racism in my own country. I know there are numerous problems I'm not yet aware of, and I acknowledge the flaws of my language—both Polish and English. But I must face it.

This is the time to change the minds of my people—and not only my people. I must take the risk of waking up members of the Black nation. It *is* our time to be—and perhaps there won't be another.

Wrocław, August 2, 2024
On the hundredth anniversary of James Baldwin's birth

---

3 See: F. Fanon, *Black Skin, White Masks*, 111.

Part I

Blacks and Poles

When one is raised as a Black Pole, one learns that Africa has no history, and neither do they. It means, among other things, that in Polish history books, it's difficult to find a person who has been both African and Polish, in any sense. In school textbooks, there is no such person. That is why, during my childhood and teenage years, I believed I was alone in a historic sense; I believed there was no historical figure I could take an example from. It takes a lot of time—too much time, I shall say—and maturity and will to learn about those great, metaphorical ancestors, to find them, and to understand that you're not the first nor the only one.

It all started, as far as I know, in the eighteenth century with Mmadi Make, also known as Angelo Soliman, an African Austrian Freemason. We do not know whether he was born in today's Nigeria or Cameroon, but in some sources, we can find information that he was a member of the Nigerian royal family. As a child, Make was taken captive and brought to Marseille. The family that bought him took care of his education. He accepted Christianity in his childhood—or, rather, he was forced to—and chose Angelo as his Christian name. During his life, he was, among others, a royal tutor to Aloys I, the Prince of Liechtenstein. In his forties, he married Magdalena Christiani and therefore became a brother-in-law to one of Napoleon's later marshals. Soliman also became Grand Master of the True Concord Freemason Lodge, where members included, for instance, Wolfgang Amadeus Mozart and Joseph Haydn. He was a friend of the Austrian Emperor Joseph II and his personal guest at his very wedding. One could say that Soliman took a long journey from being a slave to being a member of the European elite. Nevertheless, death—which should make us all equal, as many claim—made him a slave again. He wasn't buried as he should have been; he did not get a Christian funeral or anything of the sort. Angelo Soliman was mummified and kept as an exotic exhibit by his friend Joseph II's successor, Francis.

But I write about him mainly because of his grandson, Eduard von Feuchtersleben, a Romantic-era writer and also a mining engineer. Eduard was born in Kraków, a former Polish capital city, during the Polish partition, under the Austrian Empire. His younger half-brother coined the word "psychosis."

There's also George Bridgetower, a great violinist, to mention, British by choice, born in Biała Podlaska in Poland. He was a good friend of Ludwig van Beethoven, who dedicated Violin Sonata No. 9 to him and admired his skills. It's said that their friendship was later broken off due to a disagreement about a woman—one of the pieces of evidence is the fact that the piece originally dedicated to Bridgetower had been re-dedicated by van Beethoven to another violinist, Rodolphe Kreutzer, and today is known as the Kreutzer Sonata.

Perhaps I should start this story differently.

In the eighteenth century, it was quite fashionable among Polish noblemen to bring African servants to their properties. In this way, they were showing off their wealth and power. Like many things that were praised by the Polish upper class, this fashion came from Western manors. For example, in Warsaw's manor of Izabela Czartoryska Lubomirska, a member of two most powerful aristocratic families in then-Poland, there was "Negro Ambrose." Even King Stanisław August Poniatowski, the last monarch of independent Poland, had several African and Black servants—we know, for instance, about Jean Ledoux, who served the king from the beginning of his rule. They were immortalized by Bernardo Bellotto, known as Canaletto Jr., in his paintings. But the role of Blacks in Poland during those times wasn't limited to being a servant. There is a record from 1795, the last year of existence of the First Republic, about Katarzyna Rohoczewska, "a Negro as if from America," who ran a grange in Vilnius (Wilno), today's capital city of Lithuania.

One can assume, therefore, that Tadeusz Kościuszko met a Black at the latest in 1765, when as a nineteen-year-old man, he joined the Warsaw Corps of Cadets. The young student—who would later become a general, gained the trust and respect of George Washington, befriended Thomas Jefferson, and was considered a national hero of both Poland and the United States—had been reading writers and philosophers of the Enlightenment. In his library, there were books written by Thomas Raynal, a French Catholic priest and man of letters, who advocated against slavery, and young Kościuszko found his argument irresistible. While in Paris, in 1776, he heard about the American Revolution and decided to join the thirteen colonies. During the Revolution, Kościuszko met, among others, Mihisihkinaahkwa, also known as Little Turtle, a Sagamore (Chief) of the Miami people, to whom he gave several guns saying, "Use it against anyone who will threaten your people." Kościuszko also encountered a few Founding Fathers, including the abovementioned George Washington and Thomas Jefferson. In 1783, the American Congress appointed Kościuszko as a brevet U.S. brigadier general. After the American Revolution, Kościuszko returned to Europe, and after Poland was torn apart by Russia, Prussia, and Austria, he led the rebellion named in his honor. During his lifetime, Kościuszko became a hero of three sonnets written, interestingly, by English poets: Samuel Taylor Coleridge, Leigh Hunt, and John Keats (all called *To Kosciusko*).

While serving in the American army, Kościuszko met eighteen-year-old Agrippa Hull, a Black free man who decided to join the army, despite the fact that it was primarily prohibited for Blacks to do so. Hull eventually became an adjutant of Kościuszko. They even partied together. After the Revolution, Hull stayed in the United States, and Kościuszko returned to Europe, supposedly with another Black man called John. There he met, among others, Thomas Dumas, a Black French general and father of Alexandre Dumas. Then, during the Kościuszko Uprising, he had another adjutant—Jean Lapierre, also known as Domingo, a Black man. When he was wounded, Kościuszko was captured by the Russians. And what could Lapierre do? He could, after all, flee, since he wasn't on the battlefield. But no—Lapierre decided to join the general. They spent two years in the Russian prison. Later, they traveled to Sweden, and that was the end of their cooperation—Kościuszko went to England, and Lapierre returned to Poland. He became a significant worker of Duke Dominik Radziwiłł. It is written in the records of his visit to Sławacinek that he was a well-educated polyglot and was handsome as well. Lapierre could go to France or the United States, or wherever he pleased—but his country of choice was Poland.

I suppose that those encounters, along with what Kościuszko saw during the American Revolution, his readings in youth and his deep attachment to the ideas that propelled Enlightenment revolutions—liberty, equality, brotherhood—made him spend his allowance for serving in the American army on freeing Black slaves and providing them with education. That was in 1798. In the same year, in his last will, he stated, "I beg Mister Jefferson that in case I should die without will or testament he should buy out of my money so many Negroes and free them, that the restart sum should be sufficient to give them education and provide for their maintenance." Thomas Jefferson, the author of the Declaration of Independence, the third American president, and—let's not forget—a slave owner, did not act upon the wish of his friend. And, what even better shows the roots of the United States; he did not act upon his own words: "We hold these truths to be self-evident, that all men are created equal."

Another Black individual connected to Kościuszko—although I am not sure if they actually met—was Władysław Franciszek Jabłonowski, the first Polish general of African origin. He was born out of wedlock—his father was an African butler to his mother. Yet, General Konstanty Aleksander Jabłonowski adopted him. As a teenager, he studied at a French military school, where he befriended Napoleon. He served during Tadeusz Kościuszko's uprising, the very first uprising against the invaders. Like many other Polish soldiers, he later joined the Polish Legions in Italy, established by General Jan Henryk Dąbrowski, who is mentioned in the chorus of the Polish anthem. It was there that Jabłonowski Jr. became a general. The alliance with Napoleon was seen as a means to an end, and an end was independent Poland. Despite this, in 1801, he was sent to Haiti to stifle the revolution that had taken place there. Tragically, he died too early to see his Polish comrades switching sides and supporting the Haitian fight for freedom against French colonizers. Władysław Franciszek Jabłonowski is, as far as I know, the first Black person mentioned by name in Polish literature: Adam Mickiewicz wrote about him ("There, chief routs the Negroes and misses the homeland") in *Pan Tadeusz* (*Sir Thaddeus*), one of the most important—if not *the* most important—books in the history of Polish literature. Moreover, he is the first Black main protagonist in a Polish novel. In 1904, Wacław Gąsiorowski wrote *A Black General*, a forgotten tribute to Jabłonowski.

Mentioning literature, it's worth knowing that Cyprian Kamil Norwid, one of the most celebrated poets in Poland, sometimes called "the Fourth Bard,"[1] supported not only abolishing slavery but also understood the armed struggle in order to achieve freedom for slaves. In 1859, when Norwid learned about the death sentence for John Brown, he was deeply upset by that information. Because of this, he wrote the poem *To Citizen John Brown*, in which he praises Brown, expresses doubt in the "land of the free" myth, and warns America of a potential uprising by Black slaves:

---

1 The idea of national bards was established in the Romantic era by Adam Mickiewicz. Today, in Polish literary studies, there is the notion of the Three Bards: Adam Mickiewicz, Juliusz Słowacki and Zygmunt Krasiński. They're widely considered the most important Romantic poets/writers. Occasionally, Cyprian Kamil Norwid is added as a Fourth Bards, alternating with Stanisław Wyspiański (who was writing in Modernism, which is usually called Neoromantism).

Because before the song will grow, a man sometimes dies, and before the song dies, the nation will rise first.

The best known Black Pole is perhaps August Agbola O'Browne. This jazz musician, aged twenty-seven, of Nigerian origin, came to Poland a few years after it gained its independence. He married a Pole named Zofia and had two sons with her: Ryszard and Aleksander. O'Browne also became the first West African to record an album (it happened in 1928). After World War II, he worked briefly in a city hall in Warsaw, and in 1958, he immigrated to the United Kingdom, where he died in 1976. The neighbors from his time in Poland said that O'Browne was an intelligent person who spoke several languages.

But his activities during the war make him one of the heroes of my nation. In 1939, when the Nazi Germany attacked Poland—along with the Slovak puppet state led by Jozef Tiso, a Catholic priest—O'Browne fought in the Polish army and defended the besieged capital city. Five years later, the Polish underground resistance decided to liberate Warsaw from German occupation. On August 1, 1944, at 5 p.m.—known in Poland as W-hour (*godzina W*)—the Warsaw Uprising, the single largest military effort taken by any European resistance movement against the Nazis, began. It was said that the Home Army could fight for three days and then defend for another fourteen a most. It was also said that only one in twenty-six soldiers had a gun. Despite this, they fought for sixty-three days. Thereafter, Heinrich Himmler, the chief of the SS, said, "The city must completely disappear from the surface of the earth. No stone can remain standing. Every building must be razed to its foundation." And Warsaw, indeed, had been razed. It was a unique event—no other city suffered more than Warsaw in World War II. The estimated cost of losses was about 50 billion US dollars. And August Agbola O'Browne fought in this uprising, as, probably, the only Black soldier.

While the after-war government, which called itself communist but was more of a state capitalist dictatorship, had not been supportive of the Warsaw Uprising, the liberal democratic governments since 1989 have praised it. Every year, at the W-hour, a large march is held in every Polish city to pay homage to the soldiers. It's remembered as one of the most important events in modern Polish history. I suppose that the only national holiday celebrated more than this is Independence Day—and the Warsaw Uprising Day has not even been a state-established holiday. By that, I'm trying to show you how critical the uprising remains for Poles, even today, more significant than the Third May Constitution Day and other official holidays.

I was also raised to admire the uprising and the soldiers of the Home Army. So, imagine my surprise, when in my late teens—after being told that there weren't any Black people in Poland and being taught that Black people did not have a part in Polish history—I discovered O'Browne. It was an epiphany. Suddenly, I understood that I had been told lies. There is a story of Poland that has a black face, and it is an important and glorious story.

But lately, while scrolling through Twitter—or, if one prefers, X—I saw a comment stating that the memorial of O'Browne in Warsaw should be destroyed and his portrait should be removed from the Museum of Warsaw. Why? Well, according to the commentator, O'Browne was a "pathological liar and typical Negro" (whatever that means). Reading this, I was initially furious, but then I felt dejected and powerless. At that moment, I understood one thing: whoever you are, whatever you have done for this country, and wherever you have lived, you cannot be accepted in this country. Until you are white.

On the Myth of Clean Hands

One of the myths in, let's say, official Polish history is the claim that Poland has never been involved in colonialism in any way. We have never had any colonies, we have never oppressed any other nation, we have never been a historical thug—that's the most well-known version of history among Poles. Even if one wants to acknowledge the existence of Polish *szmalcowniks*—people who blackmailed Jews or Poles who were hiding Jews during the Holocaust—one can and *will* face backlash and accusations of slander. The Polish nation still believes in its sanctity—the Romantic myths of us being the Christ of nations and the Winkelried of nations[1] are still very much alive and supported by the syllabus. Could Christ or Winkelried favour colonialism? I don't think so.

But Poland did.

To understand that, we have to go back to the eighteenth century, at the end of which my country ceased to exist. First, in 1774, Count Beniowski, who considered himself both Hungarian and Polish and is regarded as a national hero of Poland, Hungary, and Slovakia, attempted to colonize Madagascar. This took place two years after the First Partition of Poland by three neighboring countries: Russia, Prussia, and Austria. In February 1774, Beniowski and his people entered Antongil Bay, the largest bay in Madagascar, and established a colony called Louisbourg, perhaps named after French king Louis XV—one should remember that Beniowski was acting as a representative of France and its absolute monarch, not Poland. (Today, the town is called Maroantsetra.) For two years, Beniowski tried to take over the island, using force and violence, as well as attempting to win over the local people. In October 1776, he was proclaimed *ampansakebe*—the supreme monarch of Madagascar, with power over all tribes. In December, Beniowski left Madagascar. Nine years later, he tried to establish a new country there—this time without and even against the French. He was killed during the struggle with them in May 1786. Fifty-five years later, Juliusz Słowacki, one of the Three Bards—the most influential Polish Romantic writers—published the poem *Beniowski*, which tells the story of the count.

---

1 Those two myths come from two romantic-era dramas. The first one, the Christ of Nations, was presented in Adam Mickiewicz's *Dziady część III* (*Forefathers' Eve: Part III*), widely considered the most important Polish drama, written in 1832. The Winkelried of Nations myth was introduced by Mickiewicz's rival, Juliusz Słowacki, in *Kordian*, written in 1833. It refers to Arnold von Winkelried, a legendary Swiss hero from the fourteenth century, who sacrificed his life in the Battle of Sempach, allowing the Swiss army to defeat the Duchy of Austria.

In 1795, the Third Partition took place, and thus, Poland was torn apart between three empires—the Russian Empire, the Kingdom of Prussia, and the Austrian monarchy—and ceased to exist. One could, therefore, say that it was itself under some form of colonialism. It didn't stop, though, the Polish colonial ambitions; at most, it slowed them down. Paradoxically, it even provided a clear, understandable explanation for Poles—we need to conquer other territories to establish a new Poland since the "original" one passed away.

A century, more or less, later, Stefan Szolc-Rogoziński, a Polish explorer born in the Russian Empire, who was studying in my home city (then Prussian), became a new colonizer—one of those born under the rule of another country. After serving in the Imperial Russian Navy, he decided to organize the first Polish expedition to Africa. Rogoziński was only twenty-one years old at the time. Among the donors, one could find notable individuals such as Henryk Sienkiewicz, the first Polish Nobel Prize laureate in Literature (1905), and Bolesław Prus, the author of *The Doll*, one of the most important novels in the history of Polish literature. The British government commissioned him as an agent in Africa.

This is how, in 1882—two years before the Berlin Conference, where Africa was divided among European countries—Rogoziński, along with Tomczek and Janikowski, entered Africa with support from Polish writers, among others.

The goal of the expedition was not only to explore Cameroon and Liberia but also to colonize and *civilize*. The desire to civilize Africans has always been an understandable argument for colonization. After all, Africans were—and still are—considered nothing but "big children," and these children need to be raised in order to become fully human. The empty and hypocritical critique of the patriarchy in African societies was part of that discourse. Janikowski, for example, wrote about double standards when it came to the sexuality of men and women or about violence toward women. He did not see this kind of discrimination against females in Europe, although it was there in his time. In 1882, very few women could vote anywhere on the earth's surface, and the women's suffrage movement was still in its infancy. However, in Africa, patriarchy was something that should be condemned. (I cannot leave aside the fact that the last European country to fully embrace women's right to vote was Switzerland—that happened in 1990 when canton Appenzell Innerrhoden was *forced* to accept women's suffrage by the Federal

Supreme Court of Switzerland. At the time, the last African country to fully embrace women's right to vote was South Africa: in 1994, *Black* women were granted suffrage, along with Black men; whereas white women could have voted since 1930.)

Janikowski also claimed, "It will take hundreds of years to establish a civilization in Africa." With his co-explorers, he tried to accelerate that process. He described, among others, the celebration of the 200th anniversary of the Battle of Vienna, when Polish King John III Sobieski, along with his army, helped Austria defeat the Ottoman Empire. It's almost a legendary battle, in which Christianity (represented by the Polish army) and Islam (represented by the Ottoman army) clashed, and Christianity won.

In the celebration, the local landlords took part—they brought presents and listened to a lecture about the Victory of Vienna, as we call it in Polish. In the end, the landlords stood up and said, "Hurray, King Sobieski!"

Yet, Stefan Szolc-Rogoziński failed to establish a strong Polish colony in Africa. In 1884, he was dismissed by the British during the Berlin Conference due to his anti-German stance. In the same year, Tomczek died. Cameroon became a German colony, and thus, the Polish colony ceased to exist. Rogoziński continued to travel through Africa for a dozen years after that. Eventually, he died in Paris in 1896, aged just thirty-five.

Approximately ten years later, Jan Czekanowski—a Polish anthropologist born during the Russian partition in the year of the Berlin Conference—went to Africa with a German expedition led by Adolf Friedrich von Mecklenburg. Czekanowski's job was to describe native races in the interfluve of the Congo River and the Nile—that is how *Forschungen im Nil-Kongo* was written.

In some sense, Czekanowski was opposing both colonialism and the poor treatment of Africans by Germans. In his journals, he draws a parallel between oppression and the difficult situation of natives; moreover, he sees connections between Poles and Africans and even calls them his "fellows." Czekanowki's position appears to be very supportive of Africans and, one could say, progressive.

Yet, he is one of the most important creators of the racial or ethnic distinction between Tutsi and Hutu. The first to propose it was John Hanning Speke who, forty-four years before Czekanowski, claimed that Tutsi are descendants of King David and argued for a distinction between "higher" and "lower" races within that society. (It's, of course, significant for me personally because of my origin. I am, after all, Burundian—or at least of

Burundian origin; therefore, this division has made all the difference in my family's story.) Czekanowski continued Speke's work, which eventually led to a civil war in Burundi and genocide in Rwanda.

Although Czekanowski wasn't a racist—or so he claimed in his diaries—his students were. Karol Stojanowski, whose grave is in my family's cemetery, was, for instance, praising a "Nordic-blond type." He tried to create a link between racial theory and politics in interwar Poland. His racial claims were critical not only of Africans but also of Jews and Ukrainians. "Poland has to be among the greatest European nations," he said—and he essentially meant what the Nazis meant. (One of his propositions was a *Lebensraum* for Poles.)

Polish colonial ambitions became visible when Poland regained independence. One of the reasons was a desire to move Jewish people somewhere outside Polish borders. It was, after all, an old dream. At the end of the nineteenth century, Germans wanted to displace Jews, and the British suggested Palestine. However, seeing the conflict between Arabs and settlers there, the search began for another place for them. (Nonetheless, as we all know, Jewish Europeans were eventually settled in Palestine after World War II.) The second reason was a claim that, due to the partition, Poland could and should demand a share of the German colonies—such as Rwanda and Burundi. Poles, having been under foreign rule for 123 years, couldn't support Africans' desire for independence—they wanted those lands for themselves. When, in 1920, William Edward Burghardt Du Bois, the great Black American and Pan-Africanist writer and activist, stated that the German losses in the so-called "Great War" could be a chance for Burundians, Rwandans, Tanzanians, Cameroonians, and others to gain independence, Wojciech Szukiewicz, a Polish essayist and translator, said Du Bois was naive. "Negro's dreams of power," he summarized. It's 1934, a year after the first of Hitler's triumphs.

One hundred years ago, in 1924, the Maritime and River League was established. It originated from the Polish Flag organization created in 1918, which was later transformed into the League of Polish Navigation. After six years, in 1930, it changed its name to the Maritime and *Colonial* League. The goal of this organization was to gain colonies for Poland. The then-dictator of the Second Republic of Poland, Marshal Józef Piłsudski, was generally against colonization; therefore, the officials did not pursue it. This dream, however, remained alive among many Poles, especially nationalists who claimed Polish superiority over Africans and argued for Poland's right to the former German colonies. "Because Poles were the one-tenth of the citizens of the German Empire," it was said, "they are entitled to one-tenth of German colonies."

When Piłsudski died in 1935, the officials of the Second Republic tried to gain territories in Africa—a Colonial Department was created within the Foreign Ministry. (Interestingly, at the same time, the first ghetto benches—a form of segregation for Jewish students—were established at Lwów Polytechnic.) Moreover, a few months after Piłsudski's death, the Second Italo-Ethiopian War began, supported by the colonial movement: "For Mussolini, colonialism is the sign of nation's vitality, justified by progress, dynamism, and the organizational force capable of *outstanding civilizational development.*" It didn't matter that Ethiopia was an ancient country, known even in Biblical times, as "civilizational development," and "European nations' vitality" meant more. Notwithstanding this, Poles, in general, weren't in favor of military intervention to obtain colonies. However, they claimed, in one way or another, that the reborn republic in Europe should and must acquire a part of Africa—because it was just. Some wanted "to be brutal and loudly demanding those territories," as General Gustaw Orlicz-Dreszer, the president of the Maritime and Colonial League, proposed in 1936, just before his death.

It was a similar line of thinking that led Nazi Germany to conquer Poland in 1939, Denmark, France, and the Benelux in 1940, and then, in 1941, to invade the Soviet Union. This is the logic of *Lebensraum*, the "living space" for the "better" nation or race. The same mindset drove Poles to fight for colonies. One cannot say that the Polish colonial movement was a marginal one, as approximately 3% of Poles were members of the Maritime and Colonial League. The belief that Europe was the center of the world and that indigenous societies could not decide for themselves was deeply ingrained in interwar Poland. What is there to say? Well, at the time, in June 1939, on the eve of World War II—during which our country was razed and our nation decimated—Jan Korolec, a Polish lawyer and columnist, claimed, among others, "The fall of national socialism isn't in the interest of Poland." Two years after this statement, he was murdered in Auschwitz-Birkenau. Fortunately, Korolec belonged to a deluded minority that believed the international socialist movement and Jews were the biggest threats. Nonetheless, I cannot forget these claims, especially since his organization still exists.

Let's go back to the Colonial League's activities. The League expressed interest in colonizing Liberia, probably the oldest African republic that has been independent since 1847. "This whole Liberia is just a play-acting state, a play-acting nation, a play-acting civilization," blasted Polish nationalists in 1935. On the table were, as mentioned earlier, former German colonies, Madagascar, and even Algeria and Oceania.

Polish colonial aspirations took a very, let's call it, practical form as well. They probably didn't notice that the time of colonial powers had ended, and Queen Victoria had been dead for quite some time—but at the time, people all around the world thought it wasn't yet the final moments of this unspoken cruelty. In 1935, Józef Beck—the same one who, four years later, would famously say, as one of the first prominent politicians of the time, "No pasarán!" to German Nazism—created a group within the Foreign Affairs Ministry to explore possibilities for the resettlement of Polish Jews. One year later, this idea was presented to the League of Nations' forum—an unusual predecessor to the United Nations. Marius Moutet, the French Minister of Colonies, declared that France was ready to welcome Polish settlers in Madagascar. Finally, in 1937, an expedition went to Madagascar to explore the possibilities for Poles to settle there. One of its members was Arkady Fiedler, a writer and traveler, whose job was to write a column for *Gazeta Polska*—a newspaper supporting the post-Piłsudski's dictatorship—about the expedition. At the very beginning of his story, he recalls a conversation between a European who had just arrived in Madagascar and a European who had lived there for some time. How did it start? One spotted a young girl. How is it going? They compared the differences between "African Negroes" and Sacalavas. I'll save you the obvious sexualization of native women, which is present until the end of the book. Yet, I cannot leave unnoticed the distinction between women and men made there: while females are perceived as attractive and full of "animal, primal sensuality," males are depicted as disgusting, brutish, and Negroid. Nonetheless, the settlers long for a white wife; after all, they believe the native women do not give their heart.

Lepecki, another expedition member, went back to Poland after ten weeks—Fiedler stayed until 1939. After his return, in 1938, Lepecki published a book called *Madagascar: Country, People, Colonization*. He took a more quasi-anthropological approach to the topic. He claimed, for instance, that there was a substantial risk of getting sexually transmitted diseases from native women and that those women were, how should I put it, very available to whites, as they believed that sexual encounters with Europeans were a kind of blessing, "which even includes their families." Lepecki also said, "Most of the native population is infected with malaria. That's the reason, without any doubt, why they are so degenerated, apathetic, and lazy, and why their children die so often."

Since his comrade Fiedler chose to write more like a traveler and adventurer—one of those we know from novels and so forth—we can immediately spot the differences between the two descriptions of Madagascar. Lepecki, as I've said, tried to pretend to be an anthropologist or scientist; therefore, the sexualization of native women or despise toward Madagascans is more subtle in his book.

Fiedler... Well, he openly wrote about the good French administration of the island that tried to civilize the savages and encourage them to work. Yet, those lazy brutes didn't care at all. He then compared Polish peasants with Madagascans: the former are hardworking, loyal, and patient; the latter, well, better not say. His book—published first as *Tomorrow in Madagascar!*— ends with a kind of credo: "I believe in Polish Tomorrow in Madagascar." After all, he claimed that only white citizens can ensure the French rule over this island full of savages trying to reclaim it for themselves.

Later, after the war, Fiedler rewrote his book and titled it *Madagascar: A Hot Village, Ambinanitelo*. Why? The new, so-called "communist government"—with which Fiedler would align himself (for example, in 1983, he became a member of the National Council of the Patriotic Movement for National Rebirth)—was not so supportive of colonialism. The Polish People's Republic was anti-racist and anti-imperialist (at least, on paper, but this is a different story).

Finally, I cannot omit the racist propaganda that was quite vivid in Poland. The most important part of it, I think, was the claim that "mixing" white Poles with "Negroes" of any kind was wrong. It went along, as it usually does, with control over the women. This means that while men's affairs with Black women were tolerated and even, in some ways, romanticized and portrayed as an example of the nation's vitality, Polish—of course, white—women were warned against Black men. The roots of this thinking were in eugenics, which later led to the Holocaust and Aktion T4. Interracial relationships and the children born from them were considered a degeneration of the race.

I could go on and on, but it's too heartbreaking. This grave awareness that, in those times, I would have been called an "accidental pickaninny" and "the sad effect of colored love," while hearing that Poland never had any colonies and has always been a tolerant country—is quite depressing.

Encounter with Communism

Four young people—two white girls, one black boy, and one white boy—are standing, smiling, and holding each other by the arms. Behind them, there is a crowd and ruins.

A black boy is giving autographs to several white individuals on Castle Square.

A white girl is kissing a black boy—or vice versa—while dancing.

Crowds are dancing on Castle Square under Sigismund's Column. In the background are the ruins of the Royal Castle.

Endless numbers of people are gathered on Parade Square, with the newly built Joseph Stalin's Palace of Culture and Science.

A white multigenerational family—from newborns to grandparents—is joined by a black man holding the baby. One of them is dressed in a military uniform.

Somewhere, a young Palestinian man stands encircled. At the time, nobody thought, I suppose, that this man would become a co-founder of Fatah, later the chairman of the Palestine Liberation Organization, President of the Palestinian National Authority, and a Nobel Peace Prize laureate. His name was Yasser Arafat.

That is what the Fifth Festival of Youth and Students—held from July 31 to August 15, 1955, in Warsaw—looks like in photographs. Its motto was "For Peace and Friendship—Against the Aggressive Imperialist Pacts." The festivals were organized by the World Federation of Democratic Youth, an international association that describes itself as anti-imperialist and leftist, bringing together mostly socialist and communist youth organizations from around the world. It still exists, with its headquarters based in Budapest, Hungary. The co-organizer was the International Union of Students, a nonpartisan association (although it leaned toward Marxism) of student organizations that ceased to exist in the 2000s. The Festival of Youth and Students was a global event aimed at engaging and connecting youth, showing their solidarity for peace and democracy, and opposing war, imperialism, and colonialism.

One should not forget what happened earlier that year.

In January 1955, the First Taiwan Strait Crisis began—the Chinese People's Liberation Army attacked the Yijiangshan Islands, two small Taiwanese islands in the East China Sea. Four days later, the U.S. Department of Defense announced that a system of intercontinental ballistic missiles capable of carrying nuclear weapons would be built. Then, the U.S. Congress granted President Dwight Eisenhower permission to use military force in order to protect Taiwan. The crisis ended in May—despite American aid, the People's Republic of China took over the islands.

In February, Iraq and Turkey established an anti-communist military organization that was later joined by Iran, Pakistan, and the United Kingdom. The United States started Operation Teapot, a series of nuclear tests, and President Eisenhower sent the first military advisors to South Vietnam.

On May 9, West Germany became a member of the North Atlantic Treaty Organization. Five days later, Operation Wigwam took place, during which the United States tested the vulnerability of submarines to deeply detonated nuclear weapons.

At the beginning of June, at the Messina Conference, leaders of six member states of the European Coal and Steel Community debated further integration, which led to the establishment of the European Economic Community two years later; this would become the first pillar of the European Union.

On the other side of the Iron Curtain, in February, the death sentence was executed in Czechoslovakia on three leaders of Black Lion 777, a secret anti-communist organization. On May 15, the Warsaw Pact—a collective defense organization of communist countries, also known as the Second World—was established.

In the Middle East, two Israeli operatives in Egypt were sentenced to death, and five others were sentenced to imprisonment due to the Lavon Affair. (Long story short, Israeli intelligence decided to plant bombs in Egyptian, British, and American buildings in Egypt, intending to blame attacks on the Muslim Brotherhood, Egyptian nationalists, or communists.) Meanwhile, in Israel, David Ben-Gurion, who was born in Central Poland, became the minister of defense. He was also the first prime minister of Israel and ruled during the 1948 Palestine War and Nakba. This didn't help with the tensions after the Lavon Affair.

This, more or less, was the international landscape looked at in 1955, just before the Festival.

Due to constant tensions happening all over the world, especially those between two super-empires—which could eventually lead to the nuclear extinction of humanity—there *was* a desire for peace. Especially young people, whose lives had just begun, were terrified by this possibility. Therefore, the motto of the Fifth Festival of Youth and Students couldn't be different—it *had to* focus on peace.

It was also the time of decolonization—only a few African countries were formally independent, British soldiers were still stationed in Egypt, and South Africa remained an apartheid state where white colonizers oppressed the indigenous people. The Algerian fight for independence just started a year before. For this reason, the ninth day of the Festival was designated the Day of Solidarity with Colonial Youth. After all, decolonization and support for African nations fighting for their freedom were part of the official line-up of the Festival.

The authorities made every effort to show postwar Warsaw, which was razed by Nazi Germany in 1944, as a new city—a socialist city. Joyful decorations were prepared, a new stadium called the 10th Anniversary Stadium was built, and bars were equipped. The goal was to showcase the young socialist republic as strong and modern—not only to delegates from Africa and Asia but also, above all, to those who came from the West.

For many Varsovians, it was the first time they had seen a real African, a Black person, or an Asian. Everything seemed exotic to them— "Negroes from Africa" and "Negroes from Brazil," their black, curly hair, their songs, their dances, and their skin. Their scent was like something unknown, and their taste was unfamiliar to anything here.

Newspapers wrote about a big costume party at the University of Warsaw, where Africans could be seen wearing traditional Kraków costumes, and Poles dressed as Black people. A delegate from Côte d'Ivoire, then a French colony, said, "We, from the place under the big sun, from the place of enormous woods, are sending greetings to you. One day, Africa will also wake up." We can only speculate whether Arafat, one of the delegates, was debating with his comrades about a still-fresh Palestinian matter, the Israeli occupation, and the Palestinian right to self-determination. Perhaps one of the topics was even the Lavon Affair.

Of course, the sublime and touching moments were counterbalanced by the racist insides of Poles. Two women, watching two tall, beautiful Africans in Kente cloths, laughed and said, "Behold! They look like monkeys of a kind! It's unbelievable that this kind of person lives under the sun!" The children born from interracial relationships were referred to as "children of the festival." Even forty years after the event, Marcin Meller wrote in *Polityka,* one of the biggest weekly magazines in Poland, "The achievements of Negro delegates were legendary—they supposedly made half of Warsaw's women happy. The power of exotics was so intense that, for a young girl, showing up with a colored boy was a success. (...) Through the grapevine, one could know that, nine months later, a substantial herd of chocolate babies appeared." Moreover, "in the country, there were circulating gossips about alleged rapes done by Negroes." Not by Italians, Germans, British, or Russians, but specifically by Negroes.

The authorities and propaganda, however, underlined the anti-racist and anti-imperialist standpoint of the Polish People's Republic and all Communist states.

Nevertheless, the official statement of the state and its acts were not always aligned. The Polish People's Republic, of course, as well as any country on the east side of the Iron Curtain, was anti-racist and anti-imperialist—on paper. Moreover, even if we can agree that People's Poland was indeed anti-imperialist (though I wouldn't be sure about that—it was certainly against *American* imperialism), no one can claim it was completely free of racism.

In 1968, the world centred on Vietnam and the Tet Offensive, and later on the Prague Spring, which ended with the Warsaw Pact invasion of Czechoslovakia. Yet, in Poland, we had our own shock—the Students' March, better known abroad as the 1968 Polish political crisis. To understand it, we must go back twelve years. Toward the end of February 1956 in Moscow, Nikita Khrushchev, the First Secretary of the Communist Party of the Soviet Union, delivered a speech titled *On the Cult of Personality and Its Consequences*. In this speech, Khrushchev criticized his predecessor, Josef Stalin, and revealed his crimes to members of the 20th Party's Congress. This event began the process of de-Stalinization in the Eastern Bloc. A few weeks later, Bolesław Bierut, leader of the Polish People's Republic and a participant at the Congress, died of a heart attack—some even say that he couldn't handle the exposure of Stalin's crimes. In June, there were the first massive protests since the end of World War II. In Poznań, approximately 100,000 workers and their supporters hit the streets due to inadequate tax collection. The government deployed the army, including tanks, against protestors. Eventually, the army started to shoot and, therefore, killed fifty-seven people and wounded at least 240. After those events, in October 1956, Władysław Gomułka became the new Secretary General of the Polish United Workers' Party and, thus, the ruler of Poland. Interestingly, Gomułka was condemned by the party—likely on Stalin's orders—in 1948 due to "right-wing and nationalist deviations." (He later denied these accusations, claiming he was an internationalist.) His rule marked the beginning of an era he called "small stabilization," better known as Polish October, which has been considered a liberalization, basically a liquidation, of the Stalinist regime. Among other outcomes, it led to the release of political prisoners, headed by Cardinal Stefan Wyszyński, then-Primate of Poland. Twelve years later, in March 1968, protests took place, mostly caused by students and intellectuals. They weren't, although, against socialism or communism per se—it happened due to a multidimensional crisis within the Eastern Bloc. At the time, the Prague Spring was already happening, giving hope for "socialism with a human face," as it was called. In 1965, three years before the March events, Karol Modzelewski and Jacek Kuroń published *Open Letter to the Party*, a Marxist critique of the Polish communist party. This essay could be considered a prelude to the March 1968 events. So, as it has been said, those protests weren't anti-socialist, but, at their roots, against censorship and the reduction of citizens' freedom. Those events were the source of anti-Semitic propaganda by the Polish government. Poles of Jewish origin were slandered, fired, and persecuted. The authorities claimed that Jews were responsible for the strikes, trying to abolish the so-called "socialist government," and were basically agents of American imperialism and Zionism. The reasonable critique of the State of Israel became an alibi for anti-Semitic, state-organized campaigns. Due to these actions, at least 13,000 people were forced to resign their Polish citizenship and emigrate. What is particularly symbolic is the very fact that March emigrants, as they're called in Poland, left from Warszawa Gdańska Railway Station—the same place from which Jews were sent to the Treblinka Extermination Camp during World War II. Among these March emigrants were notable figures such as Leszek Kołakowski, author of *Main Currents of Marxism*, a MacArthur Fellow, and Erasmus Prize laureate, and Zygmunt Bauman, a philosopher and essayist who claimed, "Zionism is a nationalism like any other," and who, in Poland, has been despised by right-wingers as a Stalinist.

First, the Polish People's Republic—or, I shall say, its government—had its moment of anti-Semitism, which resulted in the exile of hundreds and thousands of Poles who had the misfortune of being considered Jews.

Second, we should take a closer look at the actions of People's Poland toward the Romani people. Although, in the first few years after *the* war, the government ceased local acts of racism—such as in Łódź in 1945, where local authorities started to differentiate Poles, Germans, Jews, and Romani—and criticized discriminating claims of its own officials, such as the averment of the voivode of Pomerania. The last one said, among other things, "Gypsies are nonproductive individuals and therefore harmful to the state." Yet, that approach shifted around 1950, when—I suppose—racism was needed again. It was officially started due to the government's resolution to help the Romani get their own home and switch to a sedentary lifestyle. Because of their nomadic way of living, they were considered harmful and nonproductive. The idea was to create "new Romani," who are productive members of society. For twelve years, nothing really happened. In 1964, a contributing editor for "Warsaw's Life" wrote that "large groups of gypsies have stayed beyond the productivization," due to the defiance of Romani and the government's lack of firm actions. Optimistically, he added that the Ministry of Internal Affairs had begun taking more decisive measures in the spring of that year "to achieve the improvement of the gypsies' situation." Officially, everything was done to help the Romani people. Yet, they felt their freedom, culture, and lifestyle were being taken from them. Not only this, but there was also a problem with police brutality: "Citizens' Militia[2] treated us poorly, constantly checked our IDs, and sometimes hit us."

It had been the forced assimilation—just like in Canada or the United States toward Native Americans. Newspapers were presenting a negative, stereotypical image of Romani. Articles about them sound like indictments: mendicity, vagrancy, thefts, robberies, frauds, neglecting children, alcoholism, rarely murders... In 1969, Andrzej Zahuta even wrote that a Romani man who hadn't had sex with a minor under fifteen was a rare phenomenon. Yet almost ten years later, Michalina Wisłocka, a well-known sexologist and gynecologist, claimed in her *Practical Guide to Marital Bliss* that young girls can benefit significantly from their experiences being with an older partner. In France, intellectuals signed a petition demanding a review of the age of consent. Among them were such notable figures as Jean-Paul Sartre, Simone de Beauvoir, Michel Foucault, and Jacques Derrida. Why, then, was there such criticism of the Romani if, in those times, it was considered acceptable by many educated and sophisticated individuals? And how could Mr. Zahuta be so sure about his statement? I am not trying to defend pedophilia in any way, of course. It seems to me, however, like an unsupported-by-facts claim which goal is to portray a certain group in a radically negative way.

---

2 Equivalent of police in the Polish People's Republic.

Authorities could claim anything they wanted from their support for Romani activists in Western Europe. It didn't change a thing about their actions in the country. Moreover, they could claim anything they wanted about their care for the Romani in Poland, but it didn't change the reality of their violence.

The Romani and Jewish people were not the only groups who became objects of the government's propaganda. In the 1960s, officials maintained two sets of books. On the one hand, authorities condemned American racism, Jim Crow laws, and the White Citizens' Councils. On the other hand, their goal was to achieve ethnic purity, which caused brutal and terrifying campaigns against Germans, Ukrainians, and Belarusians. In the late 1940s, one of the nomenclature's representatives stated, "The suitable solution for the problem of national minorities in Poland is to create a mono-national state." This came just after World War II, the Holocaust, and Porajmos. Despite the internationalist claims of a communist movement, there were still people wanting to establish a "pure" country without any unwanted elements.

One must acknowledge that, despite all those well-meaning statements, the Polish United Workers' Party was never able to eradicate racism and, what's more, never really tried. It never went beyond the struggle of two imperialist regimes—American and Soviet—that made the African nations fight for their own freedom and independence as pawns in the inter-imperialist game. During those years, while the so-called "communists" were in power, Poles heard the propaganda about the cruelty of the United States and the dreadful colonial machine set in motion by European countries. While they spoke of Polish–African or Soviet–African friendship, on this side of the Iron Curtain, they were using similar clichés toward many minorities. It was easier to condemn American and European crimes against Black people and portray themselves as anti-racist because the number of Black individuals in Poland was marginal, and therefore, racism was less visible. But it was there— Maria Dąbrowska, a Polish writer nominated several times for the Nobel Prize in Literature, noted in her diary, "Allegedly, there was a discrete decision that physicians can perform abortions for three months after the Festival because of fears of too much friendship with colored races."

In addition, that "discrete decision"—true or not—shows the attitude, the *real* attitude, toward Blacks in communist Poland. It meant that, of course, we were against Western colonialism and American racism; of course, we opposed the Israeli occupation of Palestine. Of course, we claimed to be anti-racist, anti-imperialist, and anti-colonialist. Of course, we wanted freedom for every nation and every race. However, those claims remained what they were—only claims, not real actions.

Part II

Memories of a Student, Thoughts of a Teacher

If one returns to their school, they can be overwhelmed by memories. Walking the same corridors as a kid, seeing the same teachers, and being in the same classrooms—all of it makes a person recall, almost nostalgic. It was my experience when I started working as a teacher's assistant at my own primary school in 2022. When one looks backward into the past, one has good memories to ponder about. At that time, I thought in this way fairly regularly and wondered where all of this had gone. I mean, I wondered whether we made any progress at all, or how would all that was wretched change—and if it would happen at all.

I still remembered the ghosts—or, I shall say, the living dead—of racism, which I've been facing since I was born. It had haunted me in the very place where I worked. It had been a decade between my graduation and my employment. What had changed—if anything?

Working in my old school, I rediscovered the system.

The tragedy of all minorities, as far as I know, has been that the system we all live in was not created as a shield for the weaker but as a sword for the stronger. The stronger take up this weapon, decapitate the weaker, and remain unconcerned with the consequences—because they *can*.

We're alone, rejected by an oppressive system created to crush us. To me, the best argument in favor of this claim is that the system's role is to conserve social oppression, and it can be drawn from the simple fact that it does not want to eradicate it. If it were, teachers would discuss racism with their students. I recall my lesson with eighth graders—I was explaining the very idea of discrimination and how it affects the lives of hundreds of millions, and they told me that I was the first teacher to speak about this discrimination.

I believe that avoiding the topic of discrimination reinforces it. I, myself, never received any form of anti-discrimination education during my school years. Twelve years without a real conversation on something that has been and will be a great part of human history. Only the fact of my own situation, being Black in a white country, has saved me—as a part of a marginalized group, I had to learn something about it in order to survive. But—this is the bitter truth—if I weren't, I would probably never be as aware as I am now, or at least it would happen a bit later. It is unsetting to think about this alternative reality, and it makes me depressed. Regardless, I had to explore this strange world of discrimination on my own, without any guide, a map, or a lodestar—as well as the dozens of thousands of Poles in my generation. (Not to mention all those who came before us.) During that journey, I undoubtedly dropped plenty of bloopers—too many, if you ask me—which could be, *were*, hurtful, and could have been avoided if anyone had told me about these earlier.

The lack of proper education is the reason for unawareness and ignorance. These lead to treating the Other as the Alien. We are afraid of Aliens and hate them because they—their very existence—question the worldview that has been accepted by us—or, should be said, imposed on us. And because they are perceived as a threat, there seems to be no reason to learn about them or even talk about them. The circle is closed.

I recall two situations where I heard pupils using this slur, "Nigga," not in its Polish version but literally this English word. I spoke to both of them—the conversations were quite harsh, I have to admit—and asked if they even knew what it meant or what its history was. Neither of them could answer. They just didn't know. Only when I explained to them the racial horror standing behind that slur and why it has been used by Black rappers, they looked at me with fear and shame in their eyes and started to apologize. Well, they did not have bad intentions—they were never told before that it could be hurtful.

Of course, some might argue that this should be obvious, and I should not have to explain that. One has to remember that the Polish substitute for the word "Negro" ("Murzyn") is still considered by many people as a neutral description of a Black person. What is more, "Nigga," used quite often by rappers, for numerous Poles has no context at all, especially if they're children. Long story short, we cannot apply the standards of Western Europe or the United States to this part of Europe, which is sometimes called Central-Eastern.

I also remember the sixth grader, one of the students in my class, telling me that her older sister had a Black fiancé. But she never said anything about this to her classmates because, as she explained to me, they were quite racist. "You know," she said, "I am a bit afraid of what will happen if my sister comes to pick me up from school with her fiancé." I did not know what to say. It had, in a sense, overwhelmed me. Well, I hadn't given any answer, even to my own questions and doubts—not to speak about others'. It was quite bizarre. It had happened that what was part of my experience ten years before was still—in a kind of strange way—present in the life of a white twelve-year-old student of mine.

Perhaps I didn't notice that racism as much because I was in a position of power as a teacher. But I could imagine what she felt. I have often felt powerless to face racism, not only in my daily life but also when I was a student at the same school. Her confession made me realize how much work has to be done in order to eradicate this discrimination. One could think that nothing like that happens today, and many people truly believe that. Yet there it is—the underbelly of our societies, this silent violence.

Since my book on racism was published, I've been invited to several high schools to deliver speeches. And I've seen this bottom-line racism when I've spoken to the youth. Last time, one student in the first row quietly said—but not enough—to his colleague something about sand niggers while I was discussing the migration crisis.

Later, after the official part, I sat in the library with teachers and other panelists, and one teacher said, "Well, this kind of tolerance talk could do in our neo-Nazi group." She went on to explain that there were plenty of alt-right students in one of the grades. I was shocked. It is obvious that people have different opinions, but for God's sake, we weren't talking about whether liberalism is better than conservatism. We were talking about callous, atrocious prejudices.

I wanted to say to my students, "No, dear, they'll say nothing." I really did. Nevertheless, I understood it would be a lie and, what is more, now I know I would have been talking to a younger version of myself. Long story short, it would have been an attempt to sell a benevolent lie, not only to her but also to myself. I couldn't do that. This kind of delusion, in which many people live, was never an option.

I sighed and nodded as if I would try to say, "I understand you; I've been *there*." But still, as years before, I was the only one in the school. The only Black teacher, that's to say. There was no anti-discrimination education—it has been only Sienkiewicz's *In Desert and Wilderness*.

It is absurd—quite gloomy, one could add—that the Polish Constitution proclaims equality and tolerance, and the Education Bill claims that one of the goals of education is to teach children these values. How can it be done if we do not even speak about it? African history is thoroughly ignored until the white man brings "civilization." We do not learn about Western crimes committed all around the world. Well, a couple of years ago, a new subject emerged: history and contemporary times. However, the official handbook, instead of exploring the consequences of the Holocaust and colonialism, or South African apartheid and Jim Crow laws, says not about the civil rights movement but the movement for Negroes' rights. The author even calls it "a neo-Marxist idea."

This is how the anti-discrimination education looks in Poland: "Negroes' rights movement," "neo-Marxism," and "far left." Moreover, one should understand that in Poland, because of our so-called "communist times," which had been dependence on the Soviet Union, words like "Marxist," "Communist," or even "leftist" are still considered offensive in a sense and carry a great disgrace. They mean that you are basically a traitor.

That's why I can only laugh whenever I hear that there is no racism in Poland, or there was, but now it's dead. No, quite the opposite; it is still very alive, perhaps even more vivid than ever. And there's no help from any direction.

But I would rather not be too pessimistic, though I usually am. I have some hope. Not for serious adults, no. They are too cynical and too committed to this system, which has been crushing me all these years. I am not sure if I believe in my own generation, which I sometimes find too lazy, indifferent, and ignorant.

Nonetheless, I see a change in the eyes of people of my generation and our younger comrades. In addition, I hope that, together, we will be able to end all these nightmares and change the history of the world. Perhaps we will be able to understand and explain to other fellow humans the rainbow sign given by God and thus save humanity from the fire. I only wonder if it'll happen in time.

I do still remember the little brown girl who was picked up from school by, I suppose, her mother—a beautiful Black woman with dreadlocks. And I still wonder if all of this—the bloody night of racism—will also be part of that girl's life.

The Price of a Ticket

Since August 2021, Poland has been facing something that is widely called the migration crisis. It's been significant for my writing because the narration around that crisis was the direct reason why I've started writing about the racial struggle in the first place. This particular situation pushed me to focus on that issue and made me aware of what it really means.

On August 8, 2021, sixty migrants were staying on the Belarusian side of the border. Eleven days later, Polish border guards informed the public that no one would be allowed to enter Poland. On August 31, the court didn't agree to arrest thirteen activists who, a few days before, destroyed barriers on the Polish–Belarusian border. The same day, the Polish government proclaimed a state of emergency in this part of the country. On September 19, the first three bodies of migrants were discovered in the woods. That was the first month of the migration crisis on our border. I'd been watching, quite attentively, what was happening there.

I still remember the previous migration crisis, which took place in the Mediterranean Sea in 2015. I can recall conversations about that and all those comments on Arabic and African savages. The then-leader of the opposition, Jarosław Kaczyński, publicly stated, "They can bring here diseases that were fought here a long time ago." (Perhaps the fear of "Islamic hordes" was one of the reasons why right-wing populists won both presidential and, more importantly, parliamentary elections in Poland that year.)

Nonetheless, in 2021, Kaczyński was the informal leader of my country. No wonder the Polish authorities were so cruel toward the people on the Polish–Belarusian border. The pushbacks have been, ever since, a routine for border guards, despite raising legal and ethical questions.

Additionally, there had been a great machine of propaganda of fear and terror made by the government toward migrants. Two ministers, one of internal affairs and the other of national defense, held a press conference on state television, where they were lying about migrants. They suggested, quite openly, I should say, that those people who have been trying to enter Poland, searching for a safe home, are zoophiles, pedophiles, and terrorists. There are no women and children, ministers claimed; the vast majority, if not all of them, are strong, young males and portrayed as a threat to our security—all of them.

Sometime later, a former Deputy Prime Minister called that press conference, among others, "a part of the informative policy of the government that will be evaluated by the voters." This statement clearly shows it was all about gaining support, not about real safety. Migrants, all along, had been only the pawns in their political game.

During those days, I felt anger, despair, and powerlessness. My country, which I love, had become a real villain in my eyes. One night, I wrote a piece about that, which was the beginning of my debut book.

Later, at the end of January 2022, I had been asked by my friend, who was an activist and—I would say—a politician of a sort, to help with some legal affairs, a request I was later afraid of. It turned out to be about a migrant in one of the so-called "Guarded Centers for Foreigners." He was sick, and the authorities at the center didn't want to offer him any proper medical help. A few weeks later, I was pleased to find that this man was released. In March, the same friend asked me to explain Polish and international laws on stateless people and their possibilities of getting refugee status in Poland to her boss, a Member of Parliament, and her coworkers. Well, I haven't been a trained attorney, besides I was focused more on the theory and philosophy of law. Nonetheless, I found the request quite an interesting intellectual challenge, so I agreed. Effectively, I became a refugee rights advisor in the office of a Member of Parliament.

I can say—and it's not an overstatement—that this work has changed my life. Facing the tragedies of the migrants trapped in this hostile system, hour by hour and day by day, was depressive to an extent that could've been unbearable for many. It was an all-day job since none of us could know when the phone would ring or what news we'd hear. Nonetheless, it has been formative as well, because it made me aware of the existing underlines of cruelty in my nation—and not only mine—and showed how difficult it can be to stand firm on certain principles or positions, which are, in some sense, dissenting. I also had a great opportunity to see how this invisible part of politics works. But, at the same time, we all had to pay our dues—there were no vacations or sick days, which are normal in Poland. We just had to always be ready—not because of our boss, but because of the job itself.

One of the things that I will never forget in my life is my very first visit to the Temporary Guarded Center for Foreigners in Wędrzyn, a small military village in western Poland. I did not have many encounters with the army of any kind; I should probably say I didn't have any at all. So you can imagine my shock when I entered a military area and saw a tank—one of those that before I had only seen in movies and video games—a real tank that passed our car by inches. You can also imagine the terror of a person who, all his life, has been living in a rather peaceful country without any war within its borders or any coups, suddenly entered a state of emergency area in the Schmittian sense. I saw a wired wall and a watchtower. It made me ashamed. A modern state needs military bases. I am not denying it, but the very fact that in this place we also incarcerate migrants who, at least partially, are running away from war, and we make them hear all this gunfire every day, was for me unacceptable. In some sense, I was petrified by the cruelty of my country. We spent a few hours there, talking to migrants, listening to their stories, and wondering how we could help. In the evening, when my friend and I were going back to Wrocław, we couldn't even say a word to each other for quite some time. We needed to process what we had seen and heard. Whenever I recall those men, their faces and voices, and this gloomy atmosphere of the place, I feel fear and tremble.

On the other hand, since the war in Ukraine began on February 24, 2022, Poland has opened its border to Ukrainians. We have accepted millions of them, found places in schools, and offered flats to live in. Well, one could ask why we've not been able to do so in the case of African and Asian migrants and refugees. That is a legitimate question, but I am afraid the answer is very upsetting. We just do not want non-whites here—not only in Poland but in all of Europe. (Although to be fair, I should add that we are changing hearts about Ukrainians.)

It is annoying to have to underline the fact we can—and should—verify who enters our country every time there's debate about refugees from Africa and the Middle East, and never, or rarely, when it comes to Ukrainians. And if I do underline that, I also have to face accusations that my standpoint is inhumane, conservative, and xenophobic from border activists. Polish public discourse has been unbearable for quite some time, not only on this issue.

On February 13, 2023, after working with refugees for about a year, I joined the hunger strike begun by Nazar, one of the Iraqi migrants who was locked up for eighteen months in the so-called Guarded Center for Foreigners in Przemyśl, a city in eastern Poland near the Ukrainian border. He said, "I've chosen this way of striking because it is the only way to show my disagreement."

Earlier that year, other migrants had been striking in Lesznowola, a village under Warsaw, also in a guarded center. I had been part of a group supporting their demands. We had written a letter to the authorities, but, as one could predict, nothing happened. The strike ended without any results.

That is why, in February, I decided to take part in Nazar's strike. Back in the day, I lived in the city center in a small apartment with three refugees. Our windows looked onto a busy street and a bar, which was full every weekend. In this very flat, where the floor was quivering every time a tram passed the street and the air was trembling because of the plurality of languages, I made my decision. On Monday, I stopped eating. I did not know how long it would take or how it would affect me, both physically and mentally, but I felt it was the only thing I could do. Since I am very skinny, some of my friends and relatives were worried because they thought it would be tough and could be bad for my health. I decided not to say a thing to my little brother, my grandparents, or my aunt. This was an attempt to spare them worrying or suffering. My condition—as I've said—could be alarming for them, but at the same time, I knew I had to do it. I believed, despite all the rational arguments, that *our* strike—as Polish citizens— could change something.

On Tuesday, I felt okay. I was, of course, hungry and tired, but not as much as I thought I'd be. One of the so-called "border activists" told us they found the body of a migrant in the Białowieża Forest, located on the Polish–Belarusian border. I was terrified. The government, to cover up its deadly politics, wanted to close the forest. It was outrageous. "Mr. Morawiecki," I've written on X (formerly known as Twitter), "maybe instead of closing the forest you would talk to your fellow high school alumni[1] about the migration crisis and the situation in the so-called 'closed camps.' I would be happy to share my thoughts with you." It was probably all I could do about it, and that meant *nothing*.

We were also planning a press conference in the parliament building for Thursday. I was partially responsible for it.

That day, I was already unable to go to work as a teaching assistant. I took sick leave; thankfully, it was a winter break, and my only job was to sit and watch children play. I didn't miss much.

During those days, I wrote a manifesto for the strike. It was published and quoted in the mainstream media. The daily liberal newspaper *Gazeta Wyborcza* even asked me to comment. "I have never thought I'd be a part of a hunger strike," I said. "I couldn't imagine the kind of situation in which I would decide to take such a radical step. But it happened. Some people say, 'Why do you do this? After all, it would not give any results.' And perhaps they're right. But I feel the need to show that Nazar is not alone. And if anyone

---

1 I graduated from the same high school as the then-Prime Minister Mateusz Morawiecki.

considers this strike a meaningless moral gesture, I am afraid about the moral state of a country where one must resort to such a gesture." A reader's answer was, among others, quite ironic: "I *love* activists, who are concerned about the morality of *others.*" Well, I should emphasize that I did not say anything about "the morality of others," but only about the morality of the state. The reason I said that is because I'm concerned about my morality. It just shows what even liberal Poles are really thinking about non-white refugees.

The third day of my hunger strike has begun quite well. I was weakened, that's for sure, but still lively enough to read and write a little. In the afternoon, my African brother drove me to Ostrów Wielkopolski, a town in western Poland, where we picked up Karolina, who was striking with me. Our trio traveled to Warsaw.

Lord knows how many phone calls we received. That car, full of cigarette smoke, transformed into a makeshift call center. We spoke mostly with activists working on the Polish–Belarusian border. They were talking about the missing migrants they were looking for.

In the evening, we reached the capital city. Near one of the city's biggest squares, we were talking to the refugees and migrants, laughing and joking. I was trying to work on preparations for our press conference.

A few hours later, I was already in my hotel room, tired, and all I wanted was to go to sleep. Nonetheless, the universe had a different plan for me. My friends called and said that in the Lesznowola camp, one of the refugees fainted. What's important is that the guards would rather not enter the ambulance. We had tried for an hour or two to help that guy, and we succeeded.

The next day, I woke up before 8 a.m. I felt absolutely miserable—sleepy, hungry, and irritable. It was Fat Thursday, this very day of the year, when one feast, and everyone ate pączki (a kind of donut) and my beloved faworki (angel wings). On the streets, I had to see my fellow citizens eating all that yummy stuff. The same was true in Parliament, where the table of journalists was full of treats.

Before we entered the Sejm[2] buildings, we were searched by the Marshal Guards. They took away the posters brought by Karolina because they were deemed inappropriate—they criticized the then-ruling government.

What more can I say? We went to the smoking room, held a press conference, and thereafter, had another cigarette. I criticized the Left Party,

---

2 Lower chamber of Polish parliament.

accidentally right into the face of one of its MPs, and we split. I went to give an interview to a French journalist, while others attended a meeting at the embassy of one of the Arabic countries in Poland. I sat for an hour with the journalist in a restaurant, watching people eat around me—and I thought I would kill for a carrot. At that point, my legs were numb, and both my stomach and head ached. I knew I couldn't even drink coffee to fight off the sleepiness; it might be unhealthy.

My little brother called me—he knew I was on a hunger strike. I cannot recall now whether my mother had told him or if he'd read about it on social media. But I can remember very well the almost grave worry in his voice, when he asked me, "How do you feel?" It made me feel a bit ashamed. What should I say? "I'm well" would be a lie. The truth, on the other hand, could really upset him. I really didn't know what to say. That's why, I'm still delighted that my grandparents and my aunt had never known about that.

Going back to Wrocław (through Ostrów), the car became a call center again. At some point, Karolina and I were called by one of those well-known "border activists," as they are referred to in Poland. He told us they had just found a body. And again; and again. On that single day alone, three corpses were discovered.

Karolina was talking, and I was just terrified. This had been beyond my imagination. Well, I would be incredibly naive, blind, and stupid, if I thought that it has not been happening since the very beginning of the migration crisis. I was, at least theoretically, aware of the dead bodies found on the southern and eastern borders of the European Union. My job as MP's advisor was, partially, to explain what one should do in that case. But then, when I wasn't as I usually am, I couldn't even speak. How could I? In *my* country, three people have just been found dead just because we chose to play the wall game. We've thrown out the Europeans' ideals. It has meant that well-known human rights treaties and conventions weren't the real will of Europe but just useless pieces of paper.

The reason I was terrified was that I had to confront the cruelty of my fellow Europeans. Moreover, it meant that those who were striking could easily die, and no one would care. The world I've been living in hasn't been wonderful, friendly, or even fair. It is unlikely to change; it would rather remain hostile.

We met, along the way, one of those saved migrants from *the* border. I tried to behave like nothing happened—I really did. But I knew very well that the person I was speaking with could be dead as well. It is quite surrealistic to understand that the very person you see had been saved by something that can be called a miracle. And what is even more surrealistic—*and* terrifying—is that *you* (or your parents) could die on that same border.

Thereafter, we came back to Wrocław.

I was sleepy, but at the same time—because of hunger, sadness, and rage—I couldn't sleep properly. I was more like a napper, and the only dream I had was about eating. My body was quietly signaling that it was slowly reaching its boundaries. But it was *that* day.

I believe I was told before noon that Nazar was freed. In the afternoon, he was already on his way to my place. Then I had my first meal on Sunday. It's one of those meals one remembers quite well. It was vegetable pulp, without any flavors. Despite my hunger, I could've eaten only two little bowls of it. In the evening, we were all sitting together—joking, drinking, smoking, and just enjoying each other's company and our freedom. Karolina and Maria even bought a cake to celebrate Nazar's birthday, which took place two weeks before. The French journalist also came. I could not recall such a feast, although I ate almost nothing, full of joy and hope.

The discrepancy between the hunger strike and its end cannot be considered only as a hunger problem. My empty stomach was partially the reason I was blue those days, there was neither the only reason nor the primary one.

That very evening, I felt, in a sense, that racist migration politics does not exist. There was only our little party—not a powerful, hostile state machine. For that brief moment, we could forget about it.

It appears that the government is trying to convince people that it can prevent migration, although migration is as old as humankind itself. Yet, since authorities claim otherwise, we may and should ask: what exactly has the Polish government done to prevent non-white migrants and refugees from coming to the European Union? What has Brussels done? Well, I dare to say, nothing has been done. Migrants and refugees have been coming to the borderland but are prevented from entering our miraculous island, I shall repeat myself, of liberty, equality, and brotherhood. To end the migration crises we've been facing, we desperately need a more profound understanding of the mechanisms that created these crises themselves. Yet, it won't be possible, ever, if migration as such is still treated as equivalent to the crisis that kills people and is uncontrolled whatsoever. Nevertheless, we—European nations—have chosen to be blind to the reasons and instead focus on the results. Polish authorities, for instance, refuse to accept asylum applications unless there's a Polish witness. If not, asylum seekers are pushed back to Belarus. Why so? Because without anyone to speak up about the violations of human rights (and keep in mind that the right to asylum is one of them), and without evidence, Polish authorities feel safe to do so. As the saying goes, what one won't see won't hurt them. The rest of the European Union and its member states practice similar strategies in other places: the Aegean Sea, the Mediterranean Sea, the borders with Serbia and Turkey, and so on. Determent of asylum seekers on boats in the open sea to force them to turn back. In Poland, the asylum procedure is absurdly long, and simultaneously, nothing is done to assure that there would be less reason to migrate or seek refuge in Europe.

The Polish position in this matter is more than peculiar since Polish people were themselves asylum seekers for two centuries (from 1795 to 1989, give or take), long before the idea of a right to asylum and to seek it was introduced to international law. And now, my nation—my co-citizens, who probably have at least one migrant in their family history—has come to the forefront of anti-migration madness. Even liberals, who not so long ago supported the right to seek refuge and criticized the right-wing government in that manner, have changed their minds—or rather, revealed their true faces—and joined the voices that dehumanize migrants and refugees. The reason for that political maneuver, I suppose, was the so-called "Visagate"—then, liberals understood that the anti-migration narration would be a useful political tool, and the timing was perfect.

In September 2023, public opinion in Poland discovered that members of the then-ruling right-wing government, which had dehumanized migrants and threatened that they were dangerous, had been selling work visas around the world. They had done that in several African and Asian countries, but the symbol of Visagate, as it has been called by journalists, was India, especially Bollywood. The reason is that the public acknowledged, above all, the situation in which Indians came to Poland as Bollywood crews wanting to make a movie here. However, as far as I know, some of them later traveled to Mexico in order to enter the United States.

Now, it's being investigated not only by the prosecutor's office but also by a special parliamentary committee. We already know that at least one deputy minister was involved in this procedure. Currently, when I'm writing this, there's no trial, and no one has been sentenced—not yet.

Nonetheless, I cannot leave the terrifying hypocrisy of the authorities unnoticed. On the one hand, they have, all the time, used the migrants as a weapon in internal political struggles. The public sphere has been full of lies and propaganda—not only against migrants but also against activists who have helped them. This has been present in every government statement. The state has played the wall game, as I call it, just because it has been useful. Officially, the migrants have acted as scapegoats, nothing more. On the other hand, the same government had no issues with African or Asian migrants if they had paid a bribe. That bribe—a ticket to Europe or, as it turned out, to the United States—had its price. Well, it's perhaps too easy and obvious to say that, but I cannot resist underscoring it: the Visagate combines both the ugly, conscienceless, Machiavellian policy and degenerate capitalism.

When one has seen all those tragedies of the migrants, those dead bodies on the border, and how Poland treats the migrants, one is even more furious due to Visagate. But one should also realize that the government operates on the parody of the intentions of Jesus' words, "Do not let your left hand know what your right hand is doing."[3] It was, at the same time, a freeing experience. We didn't have to believe all the government's lies anymore. Well, I was already aware that the whole security narrative was nonsense, but it had been quite a discovery for me to realize that the authorities' dishonesty ran even deeper than I thought. In a sense, if voters were objective, it could overturn the Polish migration policy.

Some people I've met during my time in the MP's office believed that the liberal-conservative party—the biggest on the opposition side at the time—would change anything. I was more skeptical than hopeful. Its leader, Donald Tusk, also used anti-migrant clichés during the parliamentary campaign.

I've had the nerve to say that no one sane could believe anything would change in that manner. Nevertheless, we did—we had to, in order to keep up our work and not lose hope. Even my skepticism was weaker than the thought that this narration was just a political calculation, not a strong conviction. Those clichés, after all, weren't so often used.

So, when on October 16, 2023, it was announced that the government would change, and the more moderate conservatives and liberals would be in power, I hoped—God knows I hoped—our policy toward migrants would

---

3 See: Matt. 6, 3.

also change. It was political naivety that could not have been supported by anyone or anything.

Nevertheless, migrants have still been trying to enter Europe. The Deputy Minister of Internal Affairs, Prof. Maciej Duszczyk, stated that now pushbacks would be ethical, not as before. What does it even mean? I do not know. Well, if one has been to the Polish–Belarusian border, it is obvious that nothing has changed. The government is still pushing migrants back, and its only ethics is to be silent about that.

Nothing changes. We do not want any non-Europeans—that is, non-whites—in our country.

On the night of September 11, 2022, someone set fire to Challenging Hope—an old building that had been a safe haven for women, children, the elderly, and the disabled who had run away from war. It had been home to 120 people. What if any of them were not awake? What would have happened then? I do not want to think about it. I would like to not have to think about it. It would mean all those people could have died.

Since then, I have still been wondering why anyone would do such a thing. What have they been thinking? How did they explain to themselves that they were ready to commit mass murder—since there's no other way to call this act? It had to be a conscious act.

Nevertheless, this fire is only a sign of the fire that does eat our societies, and we are still not aware of it. We've become like the dog in the "This is Fine" clip. In every fascist graffiti, every racist voice, and every moment in which we tolerate the white supremacy movement. And, what's more, we claim that anyone who shows us what it means to surrender to this threat is a madman.

We, perhaps, do not know what we've been doing, but, as somewhere Susan Sontag once said, "it is not any excuse." We should know better. Nonetheless, there is this bizarre calmness. If we, anyhow, see the fire, we run away and return to the ruined places, singing: *I'm going to a town that has already been burnt down; I'm going to a place that has already been disgraced; I'm gonna see some folks who have already been let down.*

In a sense, the new center-right Polish government isn't different from the far-right one, perhaps even worse. There are no political differences between them at all when it comes to the migration crisis. The new authorities are considered liberal and progressive, so hardly anyone criticizes them for their migration policy. It is all about the state of mind of the country—and it is still very, very anti-migrant.

There are still numerous things to do about the migration crisis. It is not only about the border or camps but also about the anti-Ukrainian sentiment that is still vivid in many European countries. Nevertheless, nobody wants to speak about real solutions to the crisis, which can, at some point, bring down Europe, and nobody wants to hear about them. On the one hand, they will destroy the anti-migration narrative, which is the fuel of many far-right movements. On the other hand, they will bring down all the businesses that create the migration. This fusion of politics and capital cannot be torn up by any individual. It is quite unbreakable.

Thus, it is challenging to speak about the migration crisis in Europe. We Europeans do not care. We don't care, and we don't even want to see what is happening to people who come to European borders seeking help. I say this because I have witnessed the tragedy in the woods on the Polish–Belarusian border. I know what is happening in the Mediterranean or Aegean Sea.

At the beginning of 2022, the Polish government started to build a barrage on the border with Belarus to prevent refugees from entering Poland—180 kilometers of barbed wire. The officials claim it's necessary to protect both Poland and the European Union from helpless people who only need aid. These are people fleeing their governments, wars, and humanitarian or ecological catastrophes. And that statement is, more or less, supported by EU authorities like Frontex and even the European Commission. It is not paranoia of some sort; we can see it in Europe's south. Just read *Lesbos, Shame of Europe*, and you will also see combat ships shooting at refugee boats.

Furthermore, the United Kingdom—this ugly monarchy with a history of colonialism so obvious and well-known that there's no need to explain it further—had a weird plan to deport every migrant, despite their nationality or citizenship, to Rwanda. An agreement between the former colonizer and the formerly colonized country (which was initially a German colony and later a Belgian one) states that Great Britain will pay at least 370 million pounds to Rwanda. Not only does the European Court of Human Rights have its reservations, but so do the UK Supreme Court and House of Lords. It might be that one is Palestinian, or Haitian, or even Albanian—it doesn't matter; they all could end up in a small African country. Luckily, neither Boris Johnson nor Liz Truss nor Rishi Sunak were able to apply this deal while prime minister. After the 2024 parliamentary elections were won by the Labour Party, Keir Starmer, the new prime minister, announced that the plan would be cancelled and replaced by the newly created Border Security Command.

So, this is not only a Polish or Eastern European problem—it's a European problem. Our home's foundation is built—as I've said many times—on racism and xenophobia. We do not want Black people, we do not want Muslims, and we do not want the Other of any kind in our place. Europe, this small island of wealth and human rights, is unimaginably hostile to outsiders of any sort. Our ideals are just empty slogans. We aren't faithful to our perfection. Europeans want to believe in liberty, equality, and brotherhood, but they don't truly believe in them. If we believed, there would be no dead refugees.

How can we proclaim ourselves as protectors of human rights when our civilization kills people? How can we condemn dictatorships if we are no better? Of course, Europe pretends to be better than anyone else—any other country or region on the globe—but that is a lie. A lie that has built the world we live in.

This particular lie was the founding myth of European civilization and also of the European Union. We have trusted it, and we do still trust it. Otherwise, we must acknowledge that we are monsters. We are leaving people, seeking help, and they're dying because we would rather not do anything about it. The truth is that white people—white Europeans—would not want to be Black here. They wouldn't want to be refugees here. And yet they are still telling me lies about this.

I have spoken about barriers. The real—and only real—problem is the walls we're building are, in fact, moral barriers.

"Being an observer of tragedy in other countries is one of the most characteristic modern experiences," says Susan Sontag in *Regarding the Pain of Others*. In the past thirty years, we have watched tragedies around the world: Iraq, Afghanistan, Rwanda, and so on. But today, we see these tragedies and wars in our countries—dying people on Europe's borders are victims of conflicts in their states. At the same time, they are victims of our callousness.

In this sense, I claim Europe's racism and xenophobia are identical with a moral barrier. Many ages ago, we'd created a gulf between us and others—Black, Muslim, Hindu, or anyone who didn't fit. And it is still very alive.

Sometimes, I admit, I am tired. Sometimes, I would rather not do anything. Sometimes, I just want to give up. But I am here today despite this. I'm here for the refugees I've met in closed camps. I'm here for those still at the border. And above all, I am here for a nameless baby whose body was found in the woods.

This essay is for that baby.

A Zone of Nonbeing

1

It was a perfectly normal day.

At the time, we were mostly discussing the Smolensk air disaster. On April 10, a Tupolev Tu-154 crashed near Smolensk, a Russian city. All ninety-six passengers died on the scene, including the Polish president Lech Kaczyński and his wife, Maria; the last president of Poland in exile, Ryszard Kaczorowski; and numerous civilian and military officials. This event has marked the Polish public debate for at least a dozen years. We also discussed the flood that took place in the second half of May. That day, Catholics were celebrating the descent of the Holy Spirit upon Jesus' apostles and his mother, Mary. In Warsaw, life was going on in its normal rhythm.

And then, suddenly, we heard the thunder.

A week earlier, on the other side of the Atlantic Ocean, the same thunder was heard. Generally, it is a fairly regular sound *there*—in the New World, the kingdom of Uncle Sam. *There*, it has been, for centuries, a normal sound, something that nobody finds disturbing. Of course, it provokes some outrage; but that outrage is temporal and comes from the wretched of the Earth, not the powerful. Yet, that is precisely why it should be even more alarming in my small Slavic country.

Officially, it is not known what exactly happened. In such situations, it is usually not known—at least when one asks the authorities. They just don't want to discuss it because they refuse to take any responsibility. It's easier to say, "It's unknown," than to admit one's own abuse of power, isn't it? But the thunder—it *is* real.

Somewhere near the place, where the Kazimierz Górski National Stadium now stands in Warsaw, on May 23, 2010, the semilegal market—what remained of the biggest European bazaar, which existed at the 10th-Anniversary Stadium and has been called Jarmark Europa—was opened. Two policemen in civvies entered that place. "A routine control," it was said by a spokesman of the Warsaw Police Department when he was asked, what they were doing there. Well, turned out that it has not been a routine control.

When Maxwell Itoya, a thirty-six-year-old shoe seller, saw the police stopping one of his fellow sellers, he tried to speak with them. Maxwell was a Nigerian-born, naturalized Polish citizen. He had a Polish wife and

Polish children. He spoke the Polish language and had lived in this country since 2002. If one believes in the Constitution and what it says ("We, the Polish Nation—*all citizens* of the Republic..."), one has to also accept that Maxwell had been a member of this Nation. Especially policemen, who are vowing to protect a legal order established by *the Constitution*, should have that in mind.

But they didn't.

What really happened? We know for sure that, eventually, Maxwell was dead.

A week before the killing of Maxwell, in Detroit, Michigan, the local police Special Response Team made a raid at 4054 Lillibridge Street. They were looking for Chauncey Owens, who was suspected of murdering Je'Rean Blake. The building was a duplex—Owens lived upstairs with his girlfriend, while Aiyana Mo'Nay Stanley-Jones lived downstairs with her grandmother. When the cops arrived, Aiyana was asleep on the couch in the front room. What happened? Well, we know for sure that the police used a flash grenade. Then a gun fired. And suddenly, in a heartbeat, the short life of Aiyana was irrevocably ended.

She was only seven years old.

Later, Joseph Weekley, the police officer whose weapon fired the fatal bullet, claimed that Aiyana's grandmother grabbed his gun, and that caused it to fire. He was charged with involuntary manslaughter and reckless endangerment with a gun. Nevertheless, after two mistrials due to hung juries, the prosecutor dropped the charges. Weekley remains free.

During the summer of 2023, Nahel Merzouk, a seventeen-year-old French boy of Moroccan and Algerian descent, was driving a rented Mercedes with a Polish license plate. He was speeding. Two police officers tried to stop him, but Nahel didn't do so. Only the traffic congestion forced him to pull over. The policemen ordered the driver to turn off the engine while aiming a gun at him. Nevertheless, Nahel was trying to pull away. One of the cops had pulled the trigger. The car did not stop—it kept moving forward until it crashed into a street sign. Although the officers provided first aid, it was too late. At least, it was the official version at the beginning.

Nahel was pronounced dead one hour after the gunfire.

Florian Menesplier, who killed Nahel, claimed that the boy attempted to run him over, and that was the reason for the firing. Who would have thought Menesplier's version would be challenged by a video? Well, it turned out he was lying—the car couldn't harm him or the other cop because it wasn't heading toward them. Later, the third passenger—the second one fled before the gunfire—stated that Nahel received several blows with a gun butt, which caused him to release the brake pedal. Since it had an automatic gearbox, the car moved forward.

Menesplier is now facing charges of manslaughter.

What all of these situations have in common is racial profiling. Maxwell, Aiyana, Nahel, and many, many more could have been killed due to the color of their skin. Someone decided—a long time ago—that we were nothing, and we shall remain so *forever*. And that decree has been enforced for centuries.

Everywhere under the sun, the state uses its power and legalized violence not only to protect its citizens from thugs and criminals but also—or perhaps above all—to protect the status quo. That is, due to the current political and economic conditions, one of the most important goals of the modern state. Of course, since power and authority were invented, they have wanted to strengthen themselves, yet now, at the "end of history," as proclaimed by Fukuyama, they use a whole range of tricks. First, authorities claim that although they use violence against their citizens, it is to protect the law and social order. Second, there is a democracy, the ruling of the people, and thus their decisions aren't really theirs—they're *the people*'s will, whatever that means.

Unfortunately, they fail to mention what this "social order" really is.

2

The thunder that was heard has been explained in two different ways.

The first version, the *official* one: During the routine control, policemen approached a group of Black individuals, and one of them tried to run away. One of the officers chased him and caught him. He was about to handcuff the running-away man when both officers were attacked by a bunch of Black individuals who were throwing stones and bricks at the policemen. There was some struggle between the arresting officers and the person being arrested. At some point, someone attempted to grab a gun. It fired, and Maxwell was shot. Later, the spokesman of the Warsaw Police Department claimed, "The officers wanted to help the wounded man, yet had been attacked." It was meant to be a between-the-line information: Maxwell died due to the riots caused by Negroes. Thereafter, more law enforcement forces arrived. A police helicopter hovered above the scene. Thirty-two people were arrested, mostly Nigerians, who probably felt that Maxwell was one of them. (Unfortunately, the Polish police and the state did not consider him to be "one of us," despite him being a Polish citizen.) The officers said, "Then, the real hell began." Four police cars were broken as sellers were throwing whatever they could—bricks, stones, chairs, and more—toward scared officers who called their fellow policemen to come. Why were they scared? They were armed and had a numerical superiority, after all. After a few warning shots and an hour, the riots were over.

The second version, the *believable* one: begins in almost the same way. Two policemen, during routine control, stopped someone. Yet, in this story, he did not attempt to escape. He wasn't even a seller. Policemen wanted to arrest him anyway. And then Maxwell approached the officers and asked, "What are you doing? Why are you arresting this man? Why are you arresting an *innocent* man?" The officer, one of them, said, "Go away." But Maxwell did not listen. He was thinking about his friend, his brother, now in chains. He just took a few steps back. And then—then, the thunder came.

The media, obviously, supported the police's version of events. They claimed that Maxwell was a criminal, like the police, and asserted that the officers had killed no one. In a sense, they were right—yet they also stated that the officers were attacked by Black individuals. (One of the headlines of the articles written about the *murder* of Maxwell was "Blacks attacked the police.")

Furthermore, almost two weeks after the thunder, *The Daily Legal Newspaper*, one of the largest newspapers in Poland, published an article titled "The Nigerian Mob: Ugly Wives and Drugs." The author used Maxwell's tragic death to portray Nigerians and Africans in general as savages—here we go again—criminals, and liars. "How is it possible," the author asks, "that they are legally in the European Union?" No, it did not appear in some alt-right magazines or among some crazy nationalist journals. It was published in a respectable, liberal-conservative newspaper.

Maxwell could be killed because he was guilty—that was their message.

Guilty of what? Of being Nigerian, of being born Nigerian. Polish society has accepted collective fault and, therefore, collective punishment.

It has been fourteen years since Maxwell was murdered. The authorities—regardless of who is creating the government—still do not care. Whatever it is—liberal, conservative, or social democratic—they do not care about *us*. They have been using us as pawns in their dirty political game, and society applauds. Whatever they say, they do not really mean it. I cannot, of course, know what white people feel or what the authorities truly think. But I can assume what they feel and think by watching what they're doing. They can have a mouth full of platitudes about protecting the constitution of my country, which states, "All persons shall be equal before the law. All persons shall have the right to equal treatment by public authorities." They can sing about the land of the free and the brave and recall the Declaration that states, "We hold these Truths to be self-evident, that all Men are created equal." They can talk about proclamations, conventions, and all of those rusty papers. Yet—the grave truth, the only truth—is that those rusty papers mean nothing to them. It is nothing more than a mask that must be worn in public, that *everyone* has to wear in public. This mask is a strange one. It does not cover the entire face. Through this mask of universal rights, innate dignity, and natural equality—through all of that, we can still see either a racist or at least someone who uses racial politics in a quite Machiavellian way to achieve political goals. There is no difference between those two, though—not really. Behind both of these standpoints stands the notion of race, after all—the idea that due to the color of one's skin, one can be doomed in any circumstance and on any pretext. The desire, long story short, to be a *master*. Nonetheless, that weird mask is useful for many people worldwide. They can even be unaware that they are wearing it.

But, in some moments, we can see, with clarity that may be frightening, what was about to be hidden behind that mask—the ruthless racial prejudices or the disgraceful abuse of those prejudices.

And what about the policeman who killed Maxwell? What happened to him? Just after the murder, he took sick leave, and if one was stupid enough to believe the authorities, he went to the hospital. The spokesman of the Warsaw Police Department said, among others, "He is a young officer; he has been serving this country for four years. He has never been punished; on the contrary, he has been praised." The investigation had been opened, but from the very beginning, it was announced that this was not an act of racism. The potential charges could have been for acting *ultra vires*, which means beyond legal power or authority. Not murder, not manslaughter even—just exceeding authority. And I've said, "could have been," because, in 2012, the prosecutor closed the investigation without bringing any charges. None. Why? There was not enough evidence, at least, according to *them*.

He just walked. Just like the murder of Aiyana three years later.

3

The policeman who killed Maxwell claimed exactly the same thing as the policeman who killed Aiyana—that someone grabbed his gun, and because of this, it fired. The death has not been their goal; it just *happened*. Well, I am willing to believe in the last claim that, at the time they came to the place, they did not want the death of Maxwell or Aiyana. Nevertheless, it is not a reason for absolution. These officers had already calculated Maxwell's and Aiyana's deaths into the equation. And the result was, they *could* have killed them. And that is why I do not believe—even a bit—in the statements that anyone grabbed their guns, or, even more, that it was a reason why they *have killed* a person. And I will never believe them.

Due to the general prohibition on having a gun—at least, I suppose so—Polish police kill fewer people than the American ones. In the past seven years (and this chapter was written in June 2024), there were at least thirty-four murders performed by the police. I will not even count the corpses on the Polish–Belarusian border, which also burden the officials in my country. In the United States of America, the state that claims to be the Sheriff of the World, just in 2023, thirty-three unarmed Black Americans were killed by policemen. Nevertheless, those thirty-four murders in Poland in the past seven years are still thirty-four too many.

But, in contrast to those thirty-four murders, I cannot see any outrage over Maxwell's death. What was written by Poles after May 23, 2010? What did they say?

"One more, one more!"

"We do not want those."

"The baboon was killed, not a human being."

"IT IS NOT A PERSON."

"We hope for more 'accidents' like that!"

"I was on the scene just after the shooting and spoke with the officers who were intervening. They had information that near the National Stadium, a gorilla was raging, having escaped the Warsaw's Zoo due to fear of the flood. Black sellers wanted to protect their homie from being arrested by the officers, and the row began. One of the policemen confused the seller with the gorilla and shot him. That is all."

"I cannot believe it! The niggers are starting to rampage!"[1]

This very way of thinking—calling Blacks "gorillas," "baboons," and "savages"—makes it possible to kill any Black person in the world without any consequences. It comes from a very dark place—that is, the invention of the Negro. Since the white world has invented the notion, the idea of Negro, we cannot be safe in any sense. Our death is not unnoticed, it's *desirable*. Well, not everywhere, of course. In some places, like Africa, we are needed as cheap labor. But here, in America and Europe... Here, we *were* needed. They wanted us to work for them, to collect the cotton, to do all kinds of labor. Now, they do not need us anymore. And, since we are not needed, they want to kill us off. Just because when we are not needed, we become beasts, savages, and nonhumans to them.

It's not just a claim of some lunatics who sit in bars and, after too much booze, are presenting some racist monologs. It is not, it has *never* been a claim of a small, estranged group that spends time creating silly conspiracy theories about Negroes wanting to destroy Western, *Christian* civilization. It *is*, and always *has been*, a claim of those in power—of the majority. That standpoint has been presented by politicians, actors, philosophers, and clergymen and abused by those who have wanted to establish and fortify their own power. The wicked and disgusting claim that one person is worse than the other— that one is not a human being due to some qualities—has always been a part of the official discourse.

For that very reason, any Black person who speaks up about their struggle and anyone who points out the inner discrimination within our societies does so from, as Fanon puts it, a zone of nonbeing. Any form of our protest is a cry of the unheard, a scream of the helpless, a rebellion of the oppressed. The violence of these protests is a sign of a breakdown, a result of a sin that cries out to heaven for vengeance. It is a symptom that cannot be put into words.

I've called it, *via* Fanon, "a zone of nonbeing," since the very existence of that crime, of this sin, this radical inequality has been denied by those

---

1 See: A. Kościańska & M. Petryk, Odejdź. Rzecz o polskim rasizmie, 186-187.

who have created it. What is even more hurtful is that it is also denied by our Brothers and Sisters who want to gain the respect and blessing of the oppressor—and consequently, they claim there's nothing wrong. It is a *zone of nonbeing* because when every riot made by white men is considered the madness of a few lunatics, every riot that is made by Blacks must have something to do with the color of their skin. *Some* whites *sometimes* take part in riots; every Black always does that. When white men, wherever in the world, start an uprising, the so-called "civilized West" supports it. Yet, when the Black takes a gun and demands liberty, he becomes a criminal.

Even leaving aside all physical evidence—leaving aside the grave of Maxwell, the empty bed of Aiyana, the crushed car of Nahel, the 8 minutes and 46 seconds, the massacred body of Emmett, and Hector being carried by Mbuyisa—leaving aside all of that, the reasoning of the white world reveals what it really thinks of us. When we are talking about Eric Garner, they say, "Well, he was selling loosies." When we mention George Floyd, they respond, "Well, he was a junkie." Is it really a crime because of which one should be killed on the scene? "We will let you live," they say, "as long as you will obey, as long as you will be good."

Really? We already tried. Chris Dorner was an American soldier and Los Angeles Police Department officer who served his country. When he noticed that his fellow policewoman used excessive force toward Gettler, he reported that, officially. Dorner was Black; the officer he reported was white. What happened after his official complaint? He was fired. Thereafter, he tried his luck in the courts without any positive outcome. Okay, forget Dorner, he was a murderer after all—when nothing helped, he killed four people. Let's talk about Martin Luther King Jr. instead. He had tried to change the hearts and minds of the American people and the people all around the world. He was calm and civil all his life; so much calm and civil that he was even called "Uncle Tom." He insisted on the nonviolence principle. And what happened to him? He was *murdered*. So, does being polite and obeying really work? Forget Martin Luther King Jr. What about Medgar Evers, who used legal mechanisms—lawsuits and judges—to finish with Jim Crow? What happened to him? Did the white world celebrate him for his civil struggle with uncivil laws? No. He was *murdered* in front of his own house, with his wife and children watching him die. Forget even Evers, Malcolm X (since he was one of those who wanted a proper rebellion), and every activist who had been killed.

Tell me, what about Aiyana, Tamir, Emmett, George, Vernard, La'Mello, and Cameron? —what had they done wrong? How did *they* misbehave? Tell me, how do *they* deserve to be killed? What have they done? They haven't, they *couldn't* have done anything. They were too young to have done anything. Even then you cannot tell me they deserved to be murdered.

No, it is not about being civil, polite, or nonviolent. It is about being a Negro. And that is why Maxwell, Aiyana, Nahel, and millions of others could be killed—and that is why we could also be victims of this legalized crime. Many centuries ago, it has been decided that we are Negroes and, therefore, can be killed on any pretext. That we are nothing. Until white people won't understand this, we remain in grave danger. Because they have to answer, in their own hearts and minds, why they need a Negro in the first place. I, we ain't Negroes; we are individuals. The white world has created the concept of Negro so long ago that it does not even remember why. And it must answer that question, to understand why they stick a knife in our backs. I do not see this admission coming.

One can claim that I am bitter, and perhaps one would be right. But I didn't choose to be bitter. I was formed as a child by what I've seen and heard, and by the discovery of what it means to be a Black Pole, and how this discovery was made. I was raised seeing my Brothers and Sisters on the other side of the Atlantic being killed, and my African Brothers and Sisters being just dismissed as savages. I've been living in a place, having to prove my title to the land, despite that my great-grandfather freed Warsaw, that my grandparents were born here, and my mother, my godmother, my younger brother, and I were born in this very place. Despite the fact, this land is full of the corpses of my ancestors, and that this very land has been drinking the blood of my family for centuries. And I *still* have to prove that I belong here.

It shows what really is—at least according to the white gaze—ours, Blacks', major crime and unforgivable sin. When we dare to commit it, we are doomed. That sin is walking around the streets like they are ours, standing up, and looking right into the faces on those streets, and behaving like we have a right to live. That is our crime and our sin. The very fact we dare to embrace our own existence, and we do not condemn ourselves, is our fault that can—according to *them*—be punished by death. We can be beaten to death, put in the electric chair, or kneeled on for 8 minutes and 46 seconds. If we dare to refuse being put into the zone of nonbeing, into this limbo, well, we are in trouble. Our job is to endure that zone of nonbeing and remain silent.

I cannot recall or mention everyone who paid the ultimate price for that crime. There are too many of them. And I refuse to accept the claims that the murders of Maxwell, Aiyana, Nahel, George, or Ahmaud were justified. That they could ever be justified. That those murders are not causing the wrath of God, whomever he would have been for us.

For that reason, everybody who was sent into, as Fanon says, the real hell should be considered a hero. And I am tired of explaining to the white folks why. Enough is enough.

After the killing of Nahel, on the scene, at Nelson Mandela Square, someone left a sign that said *Combien de Nahel n'ont pas été filmés—How many Nahels have not been filmed?* And that question—the question that focuses like a lens on the outrage, grief, and horror of every situation in which one is killed by the forces of law and order due to the color of their skin—will never be answered.

And that is a very grave and tragic footnote to the very grave and tragic story.

Part III

Keep It Quiet

Lord knows how many times I've tried to understand the social standpoint through our language—through idioms, tales, and myths. Perhaps it is the only inherent feature of my writing. One can say I am obsessed, and it is true in some sense. I deeply believe the tales we have been telling ourselves are the clay from which we create our thinking about the world and—what's way more important—the unconscious or unacknowledged views of the world.

That is precisely why I find this topic so interesting and so important. How can one tell the story of Black people in the United States without understanding what "Negro" *really* means? Or how can one show racial issues in Poland, forgetting about *In Desert and Wilderness*?

So, is this desperate attempt to find my own language—and also to understand how social language affects me—only an obsession? Or, perhaps, is it something more?

Some people claim that literature—or any kind of narration—is a mirror in which we can look at ourselves. That's true in a way. There are several types of people; they share some qualities, and every type is more or less represented in literature. But it is dull to stare at oneself all the time, isn't it? What can we learn from that?

This is the reason I rather believe literature—as well as other narrative forms—is, or should be considered, above all as a bridge. Our time on Earth is limited, and no one can beat one's odds. We've got only one life. Of course, we can believe in the afterlife, but we cannot be certain. Each person is born in a particular place, in a particular culture, and at particular times, with no possibility to change it. Thus, one can think that Thomas from Milan Kundera's *The Unbearable Lightness of Being* is right when he claims, *Einmal ist keinmal*.

Here comes literature, with its variety and richness. When you learn how to read, it is like an entirely new world; a whole multiverse opens for you. As Muriel Rukeyser, the great American poet, puts it, "The universe is made of stories, not atoms." We can therefore watch nineteenth-century Warsaw in

Bolesław Prus' *The Doll*, to go inside the mind of an American slave in Toni Morrison's *Beloved*. We can see what would happen if our societies became fully totalitarian in George Orwell's *1984* or if there would be discrete, unnoticeable control as in Aldous Huxley's *Brave New World*. In short, narration of any kind makes us able to be in times, places, and frames of mind in which, in other cases, we would never have been. As Olga Tokarczuk said in her Nobel lecture, the world really "is a fabric we weave daily on the great looms of information, discussions, films, books, gossip, little anecdotes," and "how we narrate it has a massive significance."[1]

No wonder that all dictators and tyrants are afraid of storytellers—who refuse to serve them. Nonetheless, this is the desire of anyone who is in a position of power, even in democratic, liberal, and pluralistic societies. I've got the nerve to say that in the last case, it happens in a more sublime and let's say, natural way without official censors or state censorship as an open secret—thus far more dangerous for free thinkers.

Since narration is a bridge rather than a mirror, it shows what we see on the other side of the river—or what we refuse to see. (I'm tempted to claim that if literature can be considered a mirror, it's a mirror for our common blindness, fears, and prejudices.)

In *Desert and Wilderness*, written by Henryk Sienkiewicz between 1910 and 1911, is one of the first Polish novels in which Black characters appear, and the best-known one, since it has been obligatory reading in school. This adventure fiction book was written for teenagers. It tells the story of two children—fourteen-year-old Staś and eight-year-old Nel—who live in Egypt with their fathers, who are working on the construction of the Suez Canal. The children are kidnapped by Arabs due to the arrest of Fatma, the wife of Smain, and her kids by the British government. The plan is to force the colonial authorities to exchange Staś and Nel for Fatma and her children. They are taken to the Mahdi, the leader of the Sudanese Mahdiyya, and finally, they find a way to escape and try to go back to their fathers. During the journey, they meet many people—Greeks, Arabs, Swiss explorers, and many more. They even domesticate an elephant! After a long journey, Staś and Nel find an English patrol. The children return home, and the elephant is put in a zoo. At the end of the novel, Staś and Nel meet again, fall in love, get married, and, after traveling to Africa and the death of Nel's father, move to Poland.

---

1 O. Tokarczuk, *The Tender Narrator*.

It sounds, I admit, like a nice, interesting story for teenagers, doesn't it? The problem begins when we go deeper into how Sienkiewicz portrays Africans and Arabs.

First, take a look at Smain, the Sudanese caretaker, who is, practically, the source of the adventures of the main characters. He has received money from the British authorities to buy out the hostages from the Mahdists. Instead, he joins them. This is the reason for the British arrest of his wife and children. When it comes to Smain's wife, Fatma—she is the very person who convinces Chamis, a servant of Staś and Nel's fathers, to kidnap those two kids. Gebhr, Chamis' cousin, who helps him with abduction, is very cruel toward the kids.

It does not mean there are no positive non-white characters, though. On the contrary, there are, for example, Kali and Mea, servants of Staś and Nel. (It is quite understandable, though, that due to the times in which the novel's action takes place they're depicted as the main characters' servants.) They are good—yet to be *civilized*. At one point, Kali says, "If Kali steals a cow, it's good; if a cow is stolen from Kali, that's bad." This exact sentence is now part of collective consciousness as an expression: the morality of Kali. No one remembers what the narrator says after Kali's statement: "Staś was too young to understand that similar views on what's right and wrong *are presented also in Europe*—not only by politicians but the entire nations."

Compared to either obnoxious Mahdists or African (mostly pagan) savages, Staś is portrayed as a very mature, brave, and wise boy—he is almost a hero of a sort. He kills the kidnappers after he outsmarts them and brings peace between two fighting tribes, the Wa-Hima and Samburs. Then, he converts both to Catholicism and baptizes them. When Mahdi asks him to become a Muslim, he bravely defends his Christian faith. Nel, on the other hand, is compassionate and tender. She, herself, convinces Staś and Kali not to kill an elephant but to domesticate it instead.

The two main characters are quite different from each other. He's Polish; she's English. He has no country whatsoever because, at the time, Poland was partitioned between Russia, Germany, and the Austro-Hungarian Empire; she is a citizen of the biggest and most powerful empire in the world. But there, in Africa, it doesn't matter. They are white—and that makes them superior. Staś even thinks, "If I'd like, I could become king of all Doko tribes, like Beniowski in Madagascar. To come back, to conquer a large territory, to civilize Negroes."

Finally, Kali becomes king of his tribe, due to his father's death in the battle; nonetheless, first, he needs to be civilized by Staś. Even fate seems to favor Staś and Nel, as those who enlighten the dark (*nomen, omen*) tribes—two wizards, or shamans, who refuse to be baptized are eaten by a lion while stealing water supplies.

This story is not only an adventure novel but, above all, a sign of its times and a reflection of Sienkiewicz's worldview. It is not an overstatement—in the 1880s, he was, among other writers engaged in fundraising for the first Polish expedition to Africa, organized by Stefan Szolc-Rogoziński. In his *Letters from Africa*, he recounts how—to be original—he *rode* on "a Negro" instead of using a barrow. "I admit," he writes, "that I was afraid of getting dirty with my white clothes because of his black skin."[2] Is there something more to say? I doubt it.

In Desert and Wilderness couldn't have been written differently by Sienkiewicz—his worldview prevented him from doing so. When someone who finds it funny to ride on the other person just because of their skin color writes anything about Africans, there are only two possible outcomes: Negroes are either savages, needing to be civilized by white Europeans, or they are rotten to the core.

In 1935, the great Polish poet Julian Tuwim wrote a children's verse called *Murzynek Bambo—Bambo, the little Negro*,[3] the second well-known piece of Polish literature about Black people. It's about an African boy who's a diligent student but a mischievous rascal at home. When his mother tells him to drink some milk, he runs away to a tree; when she says, "It's bath time," he's afraid that the bath will change his skin color. "The little Negro is a good boy," Tuwim writes, and it is a pity that Bambo isn't "going to school with us."

And that's it—the only two well-known pieces of literature regarding Blacks. Although we have some nonfiction work written about being Black in this country, yet, to be honest, I know only three of these kinds of books—Samuel Fosse's *Black Student in Europe*, Oliwia Bosomtwe's *Like a White Man*, and mine. What's more, even foreign literature with important Black characters has not been published as often as one could think. James Baldwin's *The Fire Next Time*, an outstanding essay on racial justice in the United States, has been recently republished after almost sixty years. Toni Morrison's debut, *The Bluest Eye*, was translated only seven years ago. The first Polish edition of *Black Skin, White Masks* by Frantz Fanon appeared only in 2020.

---

2 H. Sienkiewicz, *Listy z Afryki*, XI: 331.
3 The poem is available in English on Wikipedia: https://en.wikipedia.org/wiki/Murzynek_Bambo#Text.

Perhaps this is the reason why, in Poland, we still regard this kind of literature as "racial." Around twenty years ago, when one of Morrison's novels appeared in Polish translation, the reader could learn from the book cover that she was "the greatest *Negro American female writer*." Fortunately, in most recent editions and the new translations, that statement is not present. Nevertheless, Amiri Baraka is still called "a great *Negro* poet."

Thankfully, literature is not the only way to tell stories.

"The Foster Family," a Polish TV series that I remember from my childhood, gained public acclaim and is considered iconic by some. This show was the very first one—as far as I recall—in which Black and Asian girls appeared as two of the main characters. I hate to say it, but I probably haven't seen the entire show, and all I've got are childhood memories. Nevertheless, "The Foster Family" showed me these two girls—not white, but also not foreign. That is the difference between this TV series and previous representations of non-white people, or at the very least most of them. It was the first, and perhaps last as well, time I could've related to someone on a silver screen. Zosia and Eliza spoke Polish, knew Polish culture, and attended a Polish school. Aside from their adoption and age, I really felt that they were like me.

Pop culture can be even more useful than literature in familiarizing the strange and mystifying the familiar. It is made for everyone and can be easily consumed by anyone; thus, it has greater poignancy. However, one show, finished fifteen years ago, is not enough to change the social frame of mind. It's a good clue, though, to where we, as a society, should go to.

What strikes me the most is that today, it would probably be considered by many to be a result of political correctness. "Everywhere, they must include a Negro"—that would be a reaction. This unspoken fear of any character who is not ours—this is, white—and does not exhibit any tendency toward either holiness or wickedness is a sign of the inner sickness of our culture. Holiness should be said, is usually understood as the ability to endure all the cruelties of white folks with peace and patience and without any sign of seeking revenge or even justice. A great example of that in American literature is Uncle Tom. Wickedness, on the other hand, means being a perfect embodiment of negative stereotypes. Well, at most, there can be accepted characters who need to be civilized, like Kali; that is, the character needs a white savior who will purge them with hyssop to clean them and wash them to make them whiter than snow. And that is all.

We also cannot ignore the mass culture—by which I mean absolutely meaningless and rather stupid entertainment—which happens to be one of the methods to supervise and control society in Huxley's *Brave New World*. Reality shows, celebrity culture, and so on—all of which I regard as a danger to any society. "Your Face Sounds Familiar," for example, is based on a Spanish talent/reality show in which celebrities impersonate well-known singers. And it has been repeatedly accused of consisting of blackface. Long story short, white participants have been painted to act as Black—or non-white in general—singers. Well, it is not the same as minstrel shows; nevertheless, I have been so disgusted that several years ago I did even write a piece addressing this practice. And the response I've gotten was, "Don't we experience any *real* problems?" In many ways, most Poles do not see anything wrong with it. "It's just a silly show," they say. For them, if they know what it is, blackface is an American problem, not theirs—which is why they can paint themselves black and pretend that they are Negroes.

Having said that, I should add that this issue does not apply only to television; it is also present in, for example, schools, kindergartens, and cultural institutions, such as public libraries. And rarely, very rarely, it is considered offensive.

We haven't yet understood the lessons of Western racism, and at the same time, we have been idealizing the West, especially the United States. In Poland, "the American Dream" means, more or less, paradise. Perhaps, for some people, the American system would be a divine place with happiness round-the-clock; nevertheless, I understand it *would* be a nightmare for me. In that situation, my position would be harder than before and more desperate than ever. Yet, since racial discourse has not been part of Polish evolution, we do not understand our racism, and therefore, we blindly copy certain behaviors and cultural forms without any context or more profound understanding. That is happening on both sides: for those who claim there's nothing inherently racist in blackface, and for those who simply try to transfer the American critical discourse to the Polish situation. I must admit that several times I also tried to do the latter. Now, since I have a deeper understanding of the context and history of both societies, it appears absurd to me.

Leaving aside those kinds of strange Americanization of Polish culture and our public debate on many topics, not only racism, but it also has to be said that the claim that there's no such thing as racism in Poland comes from, among others, the lack of historical education and cultural representation.

All those stories I've mentioned in the first part of this book are not present in our education. We do not discuss the colonial ambitions of the reestablished Poland. We do not have a proper representation of non-white Poles in our culture—in books, movies, TV series, and so forth. It's not anyone's concern, since it's easier to believe that Blacks have just appeared, mostly by invading Europe as immigrants. The stories of Nathaniel,[4] Maxwell, and many, many others are not interesting. Of course, we can talk about police brutality or the killings of unarmed Black Americans because it is not our problem. That means it can be used as a whip: "Look how well we treat you here! So shut up, Negro, and be grateful."

There's no place for optimism—not really. However, we must acknowledge the journey we must take. For that very reason, we desperately need new historical and cultural narratives. But to create them, we also require a new language that will be handsome, inclusive, and sharp. This is possible; we know that because it has been done by numerous writers and poets, such as James Baldwin, Toni Morrison, and Chinua Achebe. The job that is to be done is not an easy one; there are no illusions about it. Nevertheless, it *has to* be done.

I do not think waiting for someone who will decolonize the language or tear up all the racist insides of it is a sensible position. This is the challenge that stands before me and every Black Pole who breathes under the sun—to step into this forbidden territory, to endure it, and to tell everybody what we have been facing for so long. And it comes with the obligation of refusing to be defined by the language and stories that never recognized *us*.

Still, I long for the genius who will change the rules of the cultural game—the writer who will bring the Polish language to the next level, who will make it really representative, humane, and clear. I am waiting for stories in which Black characters are neither a part of the decoration nor savages who need salvation, nor Uncle Tom silently and patiently enduring the surrounding racism. I hope to live long enough to read a great novel where I will see a Black character as a real person, not just a set of superstitions, to meet the language of lean power and to consume stories of undecorated truth.

I do not know, and I cannot know—since we were all born into the losing struggle—whether any of that will happen in my lifetime. But I will try to do everything I'm able to do to make my beloved language, this fragile bird in our hands, fly.

---

4 Nathaniel was a Pole of Ghanaian descent killed in May 1997 because of his skin color.

Jimmy's Room

My first encounter with James Baldwin's writings took place in 2020. It was a warm and sunny day. After the Black Lives Matter demonstration, we went to a bar, shared a bottle, and discussed *the* situation. The police accused me, as an organizer, of breaking demonstration laws. They informed me that I would need to go to the police station—the same one where four years earlier, a young man had been killed by the cops—and testify. I had never been a suspect before, so obviously, I listened to the officers in a somewhat divided frame of mind. On the one hand, I was terrified because I didn't know what this *really* meant or what would happen to me. On the other hand, I was full of rage at the injustice and its incarnations—the cops. In those days, I still believed in the state's institutions, although I was well aware of their brutality and thought it was the fault of individuals working in so-called "law enforcement," not the system itself. Anyway, we were drinking, talking, and laughing, and I was trying to focus on the brighter side of this situation. There had been almost 500 people protesting against racism and police brutality—in such a white country as Poland, that was a colossal number. We felt that we had done something important, and we were proud of it.

I returned to my tiny apartment late. Before I went to sleep, I checked the news about protests all around Poland, and then I saw a quote from James Baldwin. I thought this was the kind of voice we needed in my country. Shortly after, I fell asleep.

About a year later, I saw a Polish translation of Baldwin's *Notes of a Native Son* in a popular bookstore. The cover was simple and beautiful; the author looked into the skies, lost in thought. I bought that book without any second thoughts. But when I finally started to read it, I could not finish. The simple beauty of the language was seductive, but the ruthless and cruel stories in this terrifying portrait of the United States left me frightened. What else would I see? How much pain would Baldwin reveal to me? I wasn't even sure if I could endure this reading.

His tough language, sharp thoughts, and the brutality of American society made me think about my own heritage. I am European. But at the same time, I am African. There is no doubt that my mother *is* Polish, and there is no doubt that my father *is* Burundian. I would rather not get on the record about my complicated "national" situation, but I must admit to being somewhere in between—both white and Black. My heritage is strange and unknown, and no one could explain it to me. I don't even think that anybody wanted to do it.

James did. He was the very first writer in my whole life who noticed me—a young Black boy struggling with his own identity. But at the same time, it *was* painful. James died before I was born. Our birthplaces lie more than 4,000 miles apart from each other. I have never been to the United States, and, as far as I know, Baldwin never visited Poland. We couldn't meet in any of the four dimensions. So, how is it possible that his experience is so relatable? Why have I had this bizarre feeling that I know him—and that he knows me, perhaps even better than my family and friends? How should I understand this closeness?

It is disturbing. It means there's common ground between a poor African American who lived in the 1940s and a middle-class African European in the twenty-first century. It means we are still waiting for the "good moment," and the ongoing change is either far too slow or just fake. Will this bloody night—a night of discrimination and suffering—ever end? James did not neglect to bring me gifts: fear and trembling.

But despite that—or perhaps because of this—I could not just forget about Jimmy. I noticed that I thought about him, I wondered what he would say, and I missed him. He became an older friend and a literary master. He has been like an older brother acting as a father and showing me stuff I needed to know to survive and understand myself. I started to read about him and watch his public speeches and interviews on YouTube. I've been looking for his books in libraries and talking about him with my friends and relatives. I've been thinking about his spoken and written thoughts, and I've believed they're mine.

It *was* an epiphany. It can sound weird, but one should know that in Poland, we do not have any writers who speak so articulately and passionately about race as Jimmy did. This remarkable encounter was, there's no doubt, life-changing because fear and trembling weren't the only gifts I received from Jimmy. He was also the first who encouraged me to seek my own language and, what's more important, told me to refuse "to be defined by a language that has never been able to recognize" me.[1] He showed me that the new inclusive language is not the demand of a lunatic but our very responsibility. Thanks to Jimmy, I was able to look for this new language. Since I met him, I have been fighting with the Polish language, trying to break its hostility.

---

1 See: T. Morrison, Life in His Language, *The New York Times*.

But, as soon I discovered, nobody knew his name. Most people around me were completely unaware of Jimmy's existence. To me, he has been a hero, a friend, someone I can rely on. To others, he was just another niche American writer, someone who might as well never existed. Perhaps I've stacked in a very unliterate group, although I strongly doubt it. We, of course, have been discussing Freud and Lacan, Marx and Luxemburg, Orwell and Woolf. Yet Baldwin was absent, along with Morrison or Fanon. They wrote about race, and that's not an interesting topic for Poles.

Once, I spoke with an English-language literature student, whom I met in a club café about books. When I mentioned Baldwin, she asked, "Who is he?" It was surprising. I understood that nobody here really cares about this part of American literature—a substantial part of it—just because we, Poles, born and raised in a monoethnic country, do not get it.

In the "Capote" movie, there is a beautiful scene where Capote talks about his lunch with Jimmy. "He told me the plot of his new book," says Truman. "He said to me, 'I just want to make sure it's not one of those problem novels.' And I said, 'Jimmy, your novel is about a Negro homosexual who's in love with a Jew. Wouldn't you call that a problem?' And he looked at me and laughed because he knew I was right. 'It's not an issue, Jimmy. Everyone's gonna be pleased with that topic!'" Of course, many weren't. But he never tried to be controversial. Jimmy spoke about the truth and cared about it—not about pleasing or shocking readers. Truth, love, and inclusiveness were controversial at this time, and they probably still are. (That would explain why we're still captured in racist thinking.)

A writer can be controversial, but that's not the goal. It is an essential lesson, especially for a young author in the era of social media, which is basically a Hobbesian war of all against all. A writer should be patient, careful, and watchful. As Jimmy was—when one watches his media appearances, one can see even his eyes speak.

I remember Maya Angelou reading a passage from Jimmy's writings. First, I thought it was a poem. His words, full of rage and pain but at the same time tender and calm, were so rhythmic, poetic, and powerful. There was something, I should say, magical about them. I felt I had faced the prophet, one of those whom I was learning about in church. His word was God's word, not in the common sense, but I felt some transcendental power in them. Only then have I learned it's not a poem; it is a part of an essay called *The Fire Next Time*.

When I read that book for the very first time, my niece was still in Africa. But I knew one day she would come to Poland, and I would be the one who would explain the racial struggle in this country to her. Back then, in 2022, she was just a few months old. She didn't speak yet; she heard Polish only when I spoke to her. But I kept imagining her as a teenager and an adult, and I thought about teaching her Polish, and how to read, and showing her all those books I'd read in my childhood. And, thanks to Jimmy, I knew what I would tell her about living in the white world.

"You can only be destroyed by believing that you really are what the white world calls a *nigger*."[2] Well, I did not know that. I never had a different perspective. All I have known in Poland was a white gaze. And suddenly, there came Jimmy, showing me a completely independent standpoint: I am a "nigger" only for them, and I will be until they think about themselves as whites. This is not *my* problem; it's theirs.

"If we do not now dare everything, the fulfillment of that prophecy, recreated from the Bible in song by a slave, is upon us: *God gave Noah the rainbow sign, No more water, the fire next time!*"[3] We are living in the so-called "interesting times," when that prophecy has been fulfilled in quite a literal way. It's the last moment to embrace our responsibilities and to end not only the racial nightmare but any kind of discrimination. Humanity must start to recognize the Other, embrace them, and be tender to the World. We *do not* have time.

And I will also tell my niece, "The very time I thought I was lost, My dungeon shook and my chains fell off."[4] That means there *is* still hope. Even when we have reached the darkest moment, it does not mean the situation is hopeless. Our task is to stand bravely against a loveless and cruel world. But hope—the mother of the stupid, as we say in Poland—is always among us.

It's something prophetic for me in Toni Morrison's eulogy for Jimmy when she says about "words every rebel, every dissident, revolutionary, every practicing artist from Cape Town to Poland, from Waycross to Dublin memorized."[5] It is unclear to me why Morrison mentioned Poland, but I treat it as a task to be fulfilled. The task, which I memorized, quoted by Morrison in her eulogy, is "Our crown has already been bought and paid for. All we have to do is wear it."[6]

We do, Jimmy. We have done.

---

2 J. Baldwin, *The Fire Next Time*, 13.
3 Ibidem, 89.
4 Ibidem, 18.
5 T. Morrison, Life in His Language, *The New York Times*.
6 Ibidem.

Time to Wake Up My Nation

One of the challenges of being Black in Poland is, as I have said numerous times, a lack of community. I believe most minorities—LGBT+ people, women, religious minorities, and so forth—have a community to turn to in their time of need. But Black Poles? We do not have it so much, not yet. It means one can be terribly alone in the struggle caused by interracial relations. For instance, the Polish Melanin Movement, the Facebook group for Black Poles, counts only 856 members. That is not even one-tenth of per mil of the Polish population. I shall repeat that there's no big or even visible Black Polish community.

Nevertheless, it exists, *we* exist. We can see each other on the streets more and more. There are also Black migrants and refugees who come here, and their kids will probably be a new generation of Black Poles.

We can also see each other in the public sphere, particularly in the streets, more and more. Whenever I walk the streets of my home place in Wrocław or whenever I visit other Polish cities, I see more Black people than ever. What's important is that they are mostly young people—my age (yes, I consider myself young) or younger. I remember when my mother once told me about another Afropean in my neighborhood: she said then, "My friend thought she saw you riding a bicycle." In some sense, it shows, as in a lens, how rare a creature is a non-white Pole, even those days. The very fact that I could be mistaken for a random boy with brown skin and curly hair should be a sufficient explanation.

Nevertheless, in the public sphere, I cannot claim that there's literally nobody.

After all, there are some actors, musicians, and sportsmen. For instance, Sara Egwu-James, a girl of Nigerian origin, was the Polish representative at the 2021 Junior Eurovision Song Contest and placed second. Furthermore, it's probably a good moment to notice that Jeremy Sochan, who plays for the San Antonio Spurs, is *Polish*-American and plays for the Polish national team as well. (Even Italian tennis player Jasmine Paolini, whose mother is Polish-Ghanaian, could be mentioned.) There have even been two members of parliament—Killion Munyama, a Zambian-born economist (now he works for the European External Action Service), and John Godson, a Nigerian-born former pastor called by his supporters "Polish Obama" (who unsuccessfully intended to run in the 2023 Nigerian presidential elections).

There's Krystian Legierski, a lawyer and LGBTQ+ activist of Mauritian origin, who co-founded the Polish Green Party and, in 2010, became the first openly gay person to be elected to a city council in Poland.

But my personal hero is the late Abdulcadir Dabeire Farah, about whom I've learned while preparing to write this book. There isn't much about him out there, especially about the first four decades of his life. He was born in the mid-1950s in Jijiga, Ethiopia, and raised in Mogadishu, Somalia (which is now its capital). That's the first gap in his biography: from birth to university. It is said that his parents abandoned him, that he was selling fruit during his primary education, and that—after middle school—with two friends and 240 US dollars in his pocket but without a passport, he traveled by foot to Sudan. This journey was 1243 miles through Kenya and Uganda to Khartoum and lasted for five months. We know he eventually graduated from Omdurman University and went back to Somalia. But what did he do there? Well, that is the second gap. In the early 1990s, due to the chaos caused by the Somali Civil War—which, by the way, continues to this day—he fled to Poland, where he became the first African refugee after the 1989 transformation and, wider, the Fall of Nations.

At the time, when capitalism and the free market were beginning to take on the status of dogma in Polish political life, an African was still a rather exotic sight. Farah recalled situations where elderly women fled upon seeing him—his black skin reminded them of the devil. It had not discouraged him, though. He became a social activist and, in 2007, with Jolanta Opalińska, Farah founded the Foundation for Somalia, which has been one of the first foundations that focuses on the Somali humanitarian crisis. He served as its president since 2010. A year later, the foundation built a hospital in Adado. Gradually, under his leadership, the foundation started to help migrants and refugees from various countries by organizing Polish-language lessons, psychological aid, and so forth.

In 2014, Farah became a Polish citizen. At this time, he started to think about running for president of Somalia, and in May 2015, he publicly announced that he would run. It is said, that his candidacy was largely approved in Somalia. Yet, we didn't get the opportunity to see if he would become the first Somali president with dual citizenship. Farah was killed in a car bomb attack on September 21, 2015, while in Mogadishu, preparing for his campaign. Nevertheless, his foundation still exists as the Foundation for Migrants "Good Start." So, Farah's legacy goes on.

We can see more Black Poles on television, and so forth; however, we cannot see more racial awareness. John Godson, for example, claimed that there's nothing wrong with the word *Murzyn*. "There's no racism in Poland," he stated elsewhere. And he said that while Maxwell was killed by a policeman, among the racist shouts. Even his colleague from parliament, Marek Suski MP, said during the Committees on Culture, Innovations, and the European Union joint session about him, "Well, your Negro votes with you" ("No, i wasz murzynek głosuje razem z wami"). Moreover, Suski was criticized even by the then-far-right journalist Tomasz Terlikowski. But no, there's no racism. It is nonsense, pure nonsense. Yet, there are, of course, organizations working for tolerance and racial equality. They, nevertheless, mainly focus on migrants and refugees who did not obtain Polish citizenship or operate under the strange assumption that Black Polish citizens must have been born in Africa.

And even if politicians, celebrities, and well-known—at least in their circles—artists, who are Black Poles, born and raised here, are willing to speak about this discrimination that cries out to heaven, they remain a voice in the wilderness. But, my dear, we desperately need those voices. Not only due to this invisible—yet painfully obvious—racism but also, I would say, to support a new generation.

As a child, I did not understand the difference between my white peers and myself. Thus, I believed there was none, convinced that no one saw the colour of my skin. I should, I admit, have known better then, since I have already had, as a child, situations where someone treated me otherwise because I wasn't white. And I still did not understand what it meant to be a Black Pole. I somehow felt that a remarkable discovery about my own identity was ahead of me, but I couldn't even guess where it would lead me and how it would affect me. Then, when I came to understand that we are not treated equally, no one could tell me that I could only be destroyed by believing that I really am what the white world—which has been all around me—calls a *nigger*. Nobody could tell me that I would face the future that I've encountered because I am black and for no other reason. No one made me aware that I was "born into a society which spelled out with brutal clarity, and in as many ways as possible, that" I am a worthless human being.[1] So, here came I, something like twenty-five years ago, yet I remained a stranger—an alien—

---

1 See: J. Baldwin, *The Fire Next Time*, 16.

ever since to my fellow citizens. That is why I did have another option than to believe I am the nigger, or, more precisely, that I'm what white people think about the nigger. That means I've started to believe it's my fault. I was unable to see when I've been treated this way because I'm Christian and when it has been happening because I've been Black. Today, I understand it a bit better than I did then.

I suppose that, in some sense, every life is a kind of forest in which we face, here and there, two roads that diverge inside of it. And, I suppose, all minorities, at a certain point, are pushed into the one less traveled. In my case, it has been the truth—since the moment I was born. And that, among others, has made all the difference. For this reason, I had to discover for myself what it really means to be a Black Pole. And it's not a pretty discovery.

Being a Black Pole means to be stuck between two worlds—here, that is, the all-the-time-wondering, "Where are you from?"—home, your birthplace, where you must defend your very right to be here; and there, the unknown home, the land of parents, but not yours. It means that you are treated as an immigrant all the time—so sometimes you feel like one. This condition—your birthright and your birth curse—comes with a question, with a constant doubt: *Who am I?* You can be woken up suddenly by a deep, terrifying, grave feeling that you have no home, your place is nowhere, and you belong nowhere—that you are unwanted. You calm yourself down, but this feeling does not go away. You are aware—catastrophically yet liberatingly aware—that many of our compatriots don't see you as one of them and want you to "fuck off back to Africa." (Back to what? To a family that isn't there any more? To unknown cities? To a language that you never heard before?)

Nonetheless, this paralyzing state of mind is not obligatory. Salvation is possible; redemption, indeed, is offered at the low price of surrendering your awareness and consciousness. If you are just willing to stay silent whenever there's racial inequality, if only you are prepared to be blind whenever the racist signs are in front of you, if you simply choose to be deaf whenever they are shouting, "Europe will be either white or none"—in this case, you will be spared from nightmares and doubts. The only way to escape from all those moments and feelings of being unwanted—the exit door, so to speak, in your hole of solitude—is by leaving them to decide about something that is your birthright.

However, whether they accept me or not, I am a Pole. This is a fact, not a topic for discussion. The streets of those cities and towns, the cuisine of this country, and Matejko's paintings, Gombrowicz's novels, Szymborska's poems, Kieślowski's films, Grotowski's theatrical performances, Mrożek's plays—all of this is a part of me, my story, my life, and my identity. Whether my fellow countrymen will admit it or not, we share the same national history, which began in 966 with the baptism of Prince Mieszko and continued through the fragmentation of the realm, the victory over the Teutonic Order, partitions, independence, World War II, and extends to this very day. Whether they acknowledge it or not, we speak the same language, with its complexities and beauty, and with its evolution from the first written sentence to its current form. And—since this world can no longer be merely black and white and never truly was—there will come a time when they'll have to at least recognize my right to be here, and my children and grandchildren will finally feel at home. I understand that one cannot always get what one wants. Yet, as Jagger sings, if you try sometimes, you just might get what you need.

This is the lesson I want to pass on to my younger Black brothers and sisters—that they do not have to accept the white Polish identity to feel at home in Poland.

After all, I do know that the world will change somehow—I'm not sure how or when, but it will. Our responsibility is to wake up members of our nation. To wake up everyone who is not aware of the ongoing racial struggle—especially those who are its main victims, that is, Black people (or non-white in general). This means we have to say plenty of things that are not wanted. We have to say what people would rather not hear. The time has come to, paraphrasing the song, wake the children up.

The time has come to acknowledge that the racial nightmare that has been an inherent part of American and wider Western history is not only their curse any more—and it never was. It has become the state of every person on the surface of the Earth. Although zones of nonbeing still exist, created by those who have been privileged, no one can claim that the racial struggle does not exist within their society. Moreover, these very zones are the sign of that struggle; that is to say, we cannot pretend anymore that we have not seen the ugly, terrifying violence going on and on. These circumstances—relationships, violence, and struggle—all of them have created a new type of human being: neither white nor Black, neither African nor European. This type has been created in the United States of America since its beginning and has been present in Europe for ages, but no one has really acknowledged it—no one who has been white. I am aware that there are still places in my country where

I would be considered a stranger (in the simple sense that no Black has been there before). Yet, whether they still exist or not, in a deeper sense, we cannot just return to a historical moment when Blacks and Whites were completely divided—I doubt that moment ever existed. They cannot pretend that I am not one of them anymore. We now live in an era where the very idea of racial division is more absurd than ever. The story of Black is not pretty, and at the same time, the story of White is not laudable. Both are indelibly linked. And they are the reason why all the suffering and wretched on Earth—sooner or later, in one way or another—will destroy the cobblestones on which the Western world is built. The world will change; it *has to* change. The party is over. Because this world has never been white, and it won't be Black either—it will be either shared or there will be no world for us.

Trouble Don't Last Always

It was difficult to write this book, not only due to the language barrier but also due to speaking of oppression, discrimination, and alienation. It is never easy, especially if it concerns *you*. For that very reason, days and nights during writing were filled with rage, sadness, and, sometimes, even despair. From dawn until dusk—or, sometimes, from dusk until dawn—every day and every night, I've had to face the fact that my country and my nation want me to be somewhere else. Perhaps because of it, I can sound like someone who, in some sense, has given up.

In times of weakness, I do want to pretend that airplanes in the night sky are like shooting stars, as I could really use a wish—a wish to eradicate racism once and for all. Yet, I do not believe—I *cannot* believe—in wishes and shooting stars. The only way to be free and equal is through action. As Toni Morrison puts it, "Look to yourself. You free. Nothing and nobody is obligated to save you but you."[1] When one realizes that everything is in our hands, and nobody else's, one can be terrified and ecstatic at the same time. There's no place for resignation or capitulation. If you want to be free, you have to liberate yourself.

But what is to be done? In these crazy times of global domination by late capitalism, times of wars, violence, and re-raising of right-wing radicalism, times of climate catastrophe, and humanitarian crises all around the globe, in times that seem to be anti-human, the answer to that question is hard—perhaps even harder than ever. Moreover, we live in an era of activism. I usually say we commit ourselves now to Thesis Eleven from Marx's *Thesis on Feuerbach*: "The philosophers have only interpreted the world in various ways; the point is to change it." The hyperactivity without any reflection—that's what's happening. On the one hand, we face circumstances that prevent us from doing anything other than encouraging and enabling us; on the other hand, we force ourselves to act, even without any theory that would support us. This almost dialectic division makes me wonder what the future of our struggle is if the two options are despair and thoughtless activity.

The very first question we have to ask ourselves is: *What do we want?* What should the world look like? What is our utopia? Well, I am aware I cannot speak for all Afropeans; I can only speak for myself. When I think

---

1 T. Morrison, *Home*, 127.

about the social and political system—and, therefore, the world—I would like to live in, I think instantly about Róża Luksemburg and what she said to her high school friend just after graduation. "My dream is such a social system in which one could love everybody without any remorse. To achieve that, and in the name of it, I am, sometimes, able to hate."[2] It's a dream of mine, too. What does that mean explicitly? The world where all those divisions, which are false and have been created to justify my slavery and, wider, the superiority of a few over the masses, do not exist anymore. A society that does not judge you based on the colour of your skin, your gender, your sexuality, or your religion. A nation that does not allow people to die on the streets just because they cannot afford health insurance. And yet, although we could make that dream fly, we still live in dystopia (think about the woman whose death went unnoticed by her coworkers for four days!), and we treat it as the only possible world. So, long story short, my ideal is to escape from this late capitalist dystopia.

Let me say again that I see myself primarily as an essayist. Not a leader of a movement, not an activist, but someone who is desperately trying to find words, phrases, and language to tell the story. I have no skills that could help with running an organization, and therefore, I cannot be an organizer, and I cannot lead the people on the barricades. My role—as I consider it—is to keep alight a torch I have been given. Endure the discrimination and describe the world in the best way I can.

Speaking about the work that has to be done to achieve *the dream*, one should also remember that the situation of Black Americans, Canadians, British, and so on—the Blacks in the so-called "Western world"—is substantially different from that of East European brothers and sisters. They've been, let's say, well-established minorities, big enough to be noticed. We, on the other hand, remain the curio, a tittle-tattle, something that does not belong here in any sense, the Stranger *par excellence*. We and they, our situations, are divided by history, culture, and language. Thus, my opinions or advice for Blacks in the Western hemisphere would be different and, at the same time, could be useless. Since I have been writing about my case, about this peculiar and particular state, in which Black people have been living in such a country like Poland for many decades, I can serve as an advisor of some sort only for them. But, I dare to claim this state is known by my brothers and sisters in

---

2 See: W. Kostryko, *Róża Luksemburg*, 50.

Ukraine, Lithuania, the Czech Republic, Russia, and so forth. In this mainly Slavic, but not only, area, the struggle is simply to say, "I am here, and I am entitled to be here."

What is to be done? I would say our primary job, as East European Blacks, is to speak up. Of course, it can be caused by my bias as an essayist. Nevertheless, I'm firmly convinced what we need is better education and knowledge in order to acknowledge the very existence of non-white Poles and others. That's the reason for my attempt to highlight, among others, the history of Black people in this region in this book. I wanted to point out that, although it's nothing compared to the Black-in-America story, we have shared the history for at least 300 years, whether my compatriots like it or not. Sometimes as friends, as enemies, but we *have*. As I mentioned countless times here, in Poland, the myth of clean hands—the notion that, since we did not have any colonies, we cannot have a problem with racism or that systemic racism doesn't exist anymore because the law says we're equal. These kinds of liberal standpoints are venomous. Therefore, our primary fight is to overcome the historical, social, political, and cultural blindness that has poisoned public discourse.

Nowadays, it appears that the main struggle has ended, as Jim Crow has been dead for quite some time. Simple gestures, like going to school or sitting on a bus, are no longer revolutionary. Yet, in Poland—but I have a strong feeling that in other countries, too—the ongoing change, the concentrated effort to liberate the minorities seem to backfire in some ways. I mean that the idea of minorities being a threat to those in power, to the privileged, is still very alive, and this time, everything, every little step, can be perceived in that manner. Black actors, characters, and so forth are suddenly treated as something weird and, more importantly, dangerous. Therefore, every step on the long road to freedom is hard. But also—every step is still revolutionary. My nation, being on this topic many decades behind the West, can still be infuriated if I say, "*Murzyn* is offensive." The conspiracy theory called Great Replacement, or even white genocide, is gaining more and more support. (The bitter irony is that whites simply fear that what they did to many nations will finally happen to them.) Well, as the French people say, "*plus ça change, plus c'est la meme chose*—the more things change, the more they stay the same."

What is most poisonous in that manner is the very idea that, since the law proclaims equality, we achieved what was to be achieved. "Thus," the proposition goes, "we do not need any liberation of any kind anymore. Everything lies in the hands of the individual, and factors such as the colour of their skin, class, or whatever else are not important. Since there are no strange fruits on the trees, since there is no segregation (at least, no official one, I would add), and since there are no death camps, we are truly equal. And everything bad that is happening to the Black people could happen to the white people." All of that is said without batting an eyelash, and I do sometimes wonder if it isn't true. I fear being grouchy—just sitting and complaining without any real reason. But I remember one crucial thing. The entire social system, historical conditioning, economic disparities, and cultural hegemony are thrown out like meaningless trash when it comes to speaking about systemic racism. And we know, too well, I shall say, that the letter of the law without applying its spirit is heartless and unjust.

But to be able to educate and, thus, uplift our society, we must first *find ourselves*. An individual, although talented, smart, eloquent, and educated, will reach the point when their voice becomes too quiet to be heard in a crowded room. What one needs, then, is firm and loud polyphony. It doesn't mean, of course, that one has to be a member of an organization or a political party; however, without the movement, individual effort is not enough to change the hearts and minds of the nation. So, how does one build that movement? Well, I do not think there's one correct answer.

What should be said is that, once again, we need to acknowledge and understand that the community that we create isn't something that we choose but rather something that we are born into—there's no escape from it. We share the same struggle and the same burden. And since that's the case, we can help each other in that—bear each other's burdens, as Saint Paul says. Solidarity, after all, is the only way to end the racial nightmare that we have been stuck in.

Building solidarity and movement is not easy, but it usually happens quite naturally. Surely, what is needed is a safe space where one can say how racism has affected them without being exposed to the white gaze. Where one won't hear, "Oh, don't be so *dramatic*," "It could've happened to *anyone*," or "Nowadays, there's no such thing as racism *any more*." Where one will get support and, what's more important, *understanding* without having to explain why this or that situation was painful. Where one will be comforted and assured that Blackness is not Ham's curse—it's rather the mark of Abel.

The movement that is yet to be born should also remember the lessons that our brothers and sisters have been taught all around the world throughout history. Cooperation between black liberation movements, especially within East Europe, is crucial. But also between East Europeans and West Europeans, Americans and Canadians, and so forth. Definitely, we can learn something from them, and perhaps they can learn something from us. This free flow of experiences, ideas, and information will be bracing. These days, the sky is the limit—there's a possibility to connect from almost every place on Earth through the Internet—the global black liberation movement can and shall exchange information and ideas and support each other's struggle.

What can also be helpful is a gathering of Black people—a Black Congress, if you want—on a national level as well as global and regional levels. After all, seeing fellow activists, writers, artists, and so forth committed to the same cause, meeting them, and talking can be nutritious.

We must not forget about the Pan-African movement. Lastly, who could help us liberate ourselves from the white gaze if not those who can assume the centrality of Blackness? We need, quite desperately, African literature, culture, and art. We require (Pan-)African activists who will tell us about the Black gaze in a Black country.

All of that is easier to achieve when organizations cooperate. Yet, we shouldn't wait until someone appears and lays the so-called "groundwork." Did Rosa Parks wait? No! She just took a seat on this bloody bus. If she did wait, perhaps nothing would have changed.

What else is to be done? Not only education and solidarity should be our weapons, after all. (Besides, as Albert Camus says, "With rebellion, awareness is born.") Let's assume, then, that the movement has arisen. What's next?

Raising the dead laws that should protect minorities is one of the priorities. Of course, trust in liberal democracy should be limited, as history has shown us its wrongdoings and mistakes. Yet, ignoring the possibility of improving—at least partially—the situation of Black people and other minorities would be reckless. The idea, after all, is to—as it was said—divide the labor *and*, therefore, the means.

So, first, we need to learn how to use the law as a weapon against discrimination and a shield that should protect us. Power, confronted with its own tools tries instantly to weaken them, yet it can still be an advantage—it shows the emptiness of Power's slogans. (To be clear, I do not mean here, obviously, that we—as the saying goes—should do business with the devil.) Showing the hypocrisy of the powerful people is part of telling people what's really going on and how to face it. This is an antidote to the poison of false liberation—seeing, once again, the emptiness of the declarations and conventions, we may be able, although only a handful, to genuinely fulfill the promise given by the law. We must embody *the spirit of the law*, not just blindly and thoughtlessly follow its letter.

Second, we must fight the politics of memory that has forgotten Black history. Leaving aside African history—since Africa appears in Polish history textbooks only when it becomes the property of Europeans—we must revoke this side of our past that is Black and oppose all strategic silencing. The time has come to include the Black minority in Poland within our historical narrative. I have tried to do so both in this book and during my lectures, especially those delivered to students. Until it becomes part of official history and the textbooks, it is our responsibility not to forget. There is also a need to revoke Polish involvement in colonialism.

Lastly, we must end cultural hegemony. After all, one must remember that culture co-creates the social state of mind. Beginning with a re-reading of such novels as *In Desert and Wilderness*, about which I've written. Until this book is presented as an unbiased account of Africans and read without the context provided by another—also mentioned—Sienkiewicz's book, *Letters from Africa*, the myth of Kali will continue to infect the hearts and minds of people in this nation. While opposing them, we must also create new stories and new myths, incorporating our existence and experience into Polish culture—through novels, theatre, and movies. We must tell stories of the so-called "Festival's Children", examine the state of mind of a Black child in an all-white society, and deal with the emotions of a Black refugee in a hostile country. At the same time, try to find a language in which it will be possible to express these stories, experiences, and emotions.

Of course, all that effort will be questioned, and it will cause panic among those whites who prefer the existing state of affairs. I can almost hear them screaming at the top of their lungs: "political correctness!"; "lies!"; "falsification of history!" (What is really fascinating is that they accuse us of the very things that *they* have done.) To be honest, I cannot wait to hear that scream. After all, it should be a sign for us that something is going in the right direction and that, somehow, change happens.

Recently I was sitting in a bar, discussing with my friends and sharing a laugh with them. At some point, the conversation moved toward the topic of racism. As usual, I tried to explain why that's so essential to me and why I decided to dedicate a great part of my writing to expressing what it means to be Black in this place at this time. Although this statement was more or less understandable to my friends, one of them concluded, "It is how it is, and we won't, we *cannot* change it." When I heard this, it depressed me at first. But then, I felt rage and dissension. There is no possibility of accepting discrimination without betraying ourselves and surrendering our birthright. No person, breathing and thinking, can take this kind of deal: you will give up on yourself, and you won't get anything in return. Well, what is wanted from us is for us to accept our captivity and move forward—it is, as Jimmy Baldwin said, a requirement "of my captivity a song," less to celebrate it "than to justify their own."[3] The demand we've been hearing since the very idea of race was born is to believe that we truly are what the white world has been calling "the Negro." Moreover, we are expected to believe in our own guilt—in the myth of Ham's offspring.

There are, as I've mentioned many times, different ways to fight this unjust and cruel world, and ultimately, it's all about the division of labour. Everyone has distinct talents and abilities that can be used; history itself proves it. One can be an organizer—like Malcolm X—and the other can be a celebrity, musician, actor, and so forth, and use one's popularity to underline the racial question, just like, for example, Sidney Poitier did. The problem is that I don't feel that I am the right person to tell them how they should do it.

While I'm finishing this chapter, in the United States, Mark Robinson calls himself a "Black Nazi" and declares his support for reestablishing slavery. This kind of Stephens—Black people who have embraced their own captivity—should and *shall* be condemned. Although I don't really believe in a blazing hell, I hope that if it exists, there's a special place for them—in the mouth of Lucifer. In Poland, on the other side of the Atlantic, neo-fascist groups are walking around the streets of cities and towns, looking for those whose skin is darker than theirs. Well, it is difficult not to be in despair, isn't it?

Yet, we cannot afford despair. We must courageously bear witness, regardless of the circumstances, until we achieve *the dream* or until the final breath. We find ourselves, indeed, in the middle of a gravely dark forest. Since sitting

---

3 See: J. Baldwin, *Dark Days*, 40.

and crying have never been an option, we have to find a way out. The people who were given a torch have the responsibility to keep it alight and show us the way. And even if the torches are not enough, we must remember what Dostoevsky said, "The darker the night, the brighter the stars."

We're tempted, all the time, to give up. We're told that the system we live in is the only possible one. And the first step to liberation is—and always has been—to refuse to believe in this claim. I won't probably see the day when liberation and equality become our reality—but the day will come. One day, the carbon stones on which the Western world, the *white* world, is built, will perish. Because as Seneca the Younger once said, "Unjust domination cannot be eternal."

Amen. Keep going.

Acknowledgments

When I sat in a flat in a prefab block near Wisła in Warsaw in December 2022, it was just after my first meet-with-author session about the book on racism in Poland that I had written. The small kitchen became a place where I met many Africans living in this country. We ate, drank, and talked. At some point, Jules—who, as far as I'm concerned, is my brother—said, "Well, Christian's just published a book." We started to talk about it, and I was telling and explaining what it means to be Black in this small republic between West and East, as it's said, at this time. Once I finished that quasi-lecture, they turned silent for a while and then said, "So why haven't you written it in English?"

Before that night, I had never thought that I would ever write something, leaving aside the entire book, in a nonnative language. Yet the direct question, followed by sincere and friendly encouragement, made me wonder: why should I not try, at least, to do so? I was struggling with this idea until I finally made it fly. Well, the first attempt was very unsuccessful, to put it mildly, but—remembering the encouragement I received—I kept buggering on. And, almost two years after my Polish-language debut, the first draft of *A Zone of Nonbeing* was finished.

It has been a long journey that I am still undergoing. I am deeply thankful to the people who have accompanied me on the road. My friends Oliwia and Alex have been wonderful supporters from the very beginning and critical readers of drafts of this book. Without the encouragement of many people, especially Jules, this work would never come into being. I'm thankful to Firoze Manji, who believed in a young, unknown essayist from some Slavic country. His suggestions, though not always gentle, undoubtedly improved this book.

The, let's say, historical chapters (*Blacks and Poles; On the Myth of Clean Hands; Encounter with Communism*) as well as the chapter *A Zone of Nonbeing*—particularly regarding Maxwell Itoya's murder—rely heavily on two great books that were published in Polish: *Odejdź. Rzecz o polskim rasizmie* (*Go Away: On Polish Racism*) by Agnieszka Kościańska and Michał-Petryk, and *Jak biały człowiek. Opowieść o Polakach i innych* (*Like a White Man: The Story About Poles and Others*) by Oliwia Bosomtwe (leaving aside numerous Internet sources). As far as I know, they are the best books available in Polish regarding Polish racism and the Blacks' presence in Polish history. The first one is more academic work focused on history combined with a modern perspective, while the second one is an in-depth reportage from an unknown area of Polish society.

To all readers: thank you for your patience and forbearance, as for my English. I hope that you learn something during our journey.

And, finally, to all fighters for equality and freedom around the world, to whom I dedicate this book: what you have been doing is important. Your words, ideas, and actions are crucial. Never forget that, to paraphrase Albert Camus, although you can be surrounded by the winter, within you lies an invincible summer.

Bibliography

Baldwin James, *Dark Days*, Penguin Books: 2018.

Baldwin James, *The Fire Next Time*, Penguin Books: 2017.

Bosomtwe Oliwia, *Jak biały człowiek. Opowieść o Polakach i innych* [*Like a White Man: The Story About Poles and Others*], WAB: 2024.

Fanon Frantz, B*lack Skin, White Masks,* Grove Press: 1967.

Fosso Samuel, *Czarnoskóry student w Europie* [*Black Student in Europe*], Wydawnictwo POLIGRAF: 2001.

Kobluk Christian, *Zapiski czarnego Polaka* [*Notes of a Black Pole*], Instytut Wydawniczy Książkai Prasa: 2022.

Kostyrko Weronika, *Róża Luksemburg. Domem moim jest cały świat* [*Róża Luksemburg: The Entire World Is a Home of Mine*], Marginesy: 2024.

Kościańska Agnieszka and Petryka Michał, *Odejdź. Rzecz o polskim rasizmie* [*Go Away: On Polish Racism*], Wydawnictwo Krytyki Politycznej: 2022.

Mickiewicz Adam, *Pan Tadeusz, czyli ostatni zajazd na Litwie: historia szlachecka z roku 1811 i 1812 we dwunastu księgach wierszem*, https://wolnelektury.pl/katalog/lektura/pan-tadeusz.html [*Sir Thaddeus, or the Last Foray in Lithuania: A Nobility's Tale of the Years 1811–1812, in Twelve Books of Verse*, trans. G.R. Noyes, https://en.wikisource.org/wiki/Pan_Tadeusz_(1917)].

Morrison Toni, *Home*, Vintage: 2016.

Morrison Toni, Life in His Language, *The New York Times*, December 20, 1987, 27.

Pitts Johny, *Afropean: Notes from Black Europe,* Penguin Books: 2020.

Sienkiewicz Henryk, *Listy z Afryki* [*Letters from Africa*], Wolne Lektury, https://wolnelektury.pl/katalog/lektura/sienkiewicz-listy-z-afryki.html.

Sienkiewicz Henryk, *W pustyni i w puszczy* [*In Desert and Wilderness*], Wolne Lektury, https://wolnelektury.pl/katalog/lektura/w-pustyni-i-w-puszczy.html.

Tokarczuk Olga, *The Tender Narrator*, https://www.nobelprize.org/prizes/literature/2018/tokarczuk/lecture/.

Titles of interest from Daraja Press

The Stories We Could Tell: Preserving The Historical Memory of El Salvador
Andrés (Drew) McKinley

From Andrés McKinley, author of For the Love of the Struggle, comes this collection of reminiscences of Salvadorans in an effort to contribute to the preservation of El Salvador's historical memory. It recounts the tragedy of a civil war that lasted nearly two decades and resulted in the loss of over 75,000 lives.

ISBN 978-1-998309-01-6 • 223 pages • $23

The Second Coming
Tariq Mehmood

In a fractured Britain, the Bloods, a US-backed Christian militia, exile Muslims to refugee camps. Marah is kidnapped by the Bloods, who impregnate her with the sperm of the dying King of England. But the Bloods have declared her baby the Second Coming. They will stop at nothing to capture him.

ISBN 978-1-998309-27-6 • 277 pages • $25

Episodes from a Colonial Present
Edited by Daniel Bendix
with work from six writers and six artists

This collective comic project deals with postcolonial critique of global inequality in everyday life in the spaces, discourses and practices of so-called 'global development'. Using the medium of comics, we take critical perspectives in a visualised form and by using everyday stories as examples.

ISBN 978-1-990263-46-0 • 104 pages • $20

Beside the Sickle Moon
Thaer Husien

A near future literary activism based on Israel's occupation of Palestine. Laeth Awad and his cousin Aylul stumble upon Israel's plans to construct a luxury hotel in their town. Aylul forms Al Mubarizun, a group crowning themselves Palestine's final resistance, but Laeth struggles with the futility of resistance.

ISBN 978-1-998309-29-0 • 167 pages • $16.99

Oh Sorry! Rituals of Forgiveness, crises and social struggles in postmodern capitalism
Panagiotis Doulos, Edith González Cruz, and Milena Rodríguez Aza

Exploring the complex relationship between public apologies, social justice, and popular mobilizations. The book focuses on Latin America but also includes a chapter on the struggles for Palestine. This timely analysis is crucial in understanding the ongoing conflicts and the role of public apologies in addressing historical injustices.

ISBN 978-1-990263-93-4 • 205 pages • $20

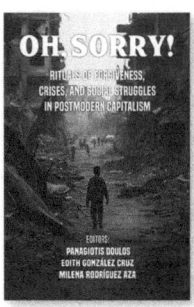

Being Anti-Colonial
Jayan Nayar

Both an invitation and a challenge to the academic community to critically revisit and re-energize the conversation about coloniality. This work stands as a pivotal contribution to academics, activists, social justice organizations, and cultural historians, urging them to rethink and rejuvenate their approach to anti-colonial discourse.

ISBN 978-1-998309-01-6 • 223 pages • $25

Weaving Our Stories: Return To Belonging – An Anthology
Luanna Peterson

Weaving Our Stories is a Hawaii-rooted abolitionist program that utilizes storytelling as a vehicle for liberation. The mission revolves around teaching storytelling as an act of resistance, dismantling harmful existing narratives, and nurturing the ability to weave counter-narratives. This anthology includes poetry, essays, visual art, and narratives penned by authors and artists who identify as Black, Indigenous, and people of color from Hawaii and beyond.

ISBN 978-1-990263-90-3 • 182 pages • $23

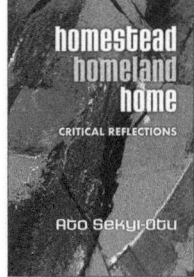

Homestead, Homeland, Home
Ato Sekyi-Otu

This book bears eloquent witness to Aki Sekyi-Otu's stature as a thinker and also to his consistent commitment to the universalization of humanity in both theory and practice. Deeply anchored in African cultures and modes of life, Sekyi-Otu has shown how ideas of human universality are ingrained in African popular sayings and proverbs and are regularly reflected in artistic creations.

ISBN 978-1-990263-54-5 • 270 pages • $19

Order from **darajapress.com**

Daraja Press